Reinventing Truth

© 2012 Edward T. Mannix, III
Published by Edward T. Mannix, III
All rights reserved. This book may not be reproduced in whole or in part without written permission from the publisher; nor may any part of this book be reproduced, stored in a retrieval system, or transmitted in any form or by any means electronic, mechanical, photocopying, recording, or other without written permission from the publisher.

Questions, comments or inquiries, please contact reinventingtruth@gmail.com.

For more information, please visit www.edwardmannix.com.

ISBN: 1-4565-7945-2
ISBN-13: 9781456579456

Reinventing Truth
A New Map of The Spiritual Path and Reality As It Is

by Edward Mannix

TABLE OF CONTENTS

Introduction.   1
Part I   11
Chapter 1.   13
The crack in the door – seeing through the most common delusion opens up a new reality
Chapter 2.   31
About the learning process and the purpose of spiritual practice
Chapter 3.   35
An essential step, mastering the victim paradox
Chapter 4.   43
Ubiquitous hidden traps and the importance of observational mind
Chapter 5.   49
Why karma sometimes isn't fair
Chapter 6.   55
Honoring healthy ego
Chapter 7.   61
Not getting lost in source
Chapter 8.   65
Avoiding one of the biggest, most dangerous pitfalls of them all
Chapter 9.   71
About gurus and the value of discernment

Chapter 10. 75
Integrating transcendence
Chapter 11. 79
Embracing aligned power
Chapter 12. 85
The importance of identifying the true source of our feelings
Chapter 13. 89
An unexpected entry point to unveil some of life's deepest and most important mysteries
Chapter 14. 107
Understanding awakening and escaping dark teachers
Chapter 15. 111
Enlightening our view of enlightenment
Chapter 16. 117
Bypassing the detachment trap
Chapter 17. 119
A special note for "spiritual" drug addicts

Part II—Commentary on Part I   **127**
Commentary on Introduction   **129**
The Great Deception; Osho and Tilopa;
Spiritual Egotism; Objective Reality and
Confusion about Physical Reality as Illusion;
The Wheel and The Spiral; Incomplete Mental Models

Commentary on Chapter 1   **137**
Fully Enlightened and Incarnate in Physical Form;
Past Lives and Parsimony; Free Will vs. Fate;
Mistakes and Perfection

Commentary on Chapter 2   **145**
Shiny New Toys and Planting Trees

Commentary on Chapter 3   **147**
Benefits of Embracing Paradox

Commentary on Chapter 4   **149**
Psychic Abilities, Spiritual Egotism and Blind
Spots; A Special Note for Healers and
Spiritual Teachers

Commentary on Chapter 5   **153**
The Delusion of Karmic Debt

Commentary On Chapter 6   **155**
Buddhism and Hinduism/Particles and
Waves; We Do Not Create Our Own
Reality (Revisited)

Commentary on Chapter 7   **161**
The Oxymoron of God-identification;
Proper Use of Spiritual Teachers and Teachings

Commentary on Chapter 8   **163**
Connecting with Your Future, Fully Enlightened Self

Commentary on Chapter 9   **167**
Confusion about Divine Will; Clearing Karma through Spiritual Practice vs. Experience in the "Real World"; When I Was Milarepa; Dangers of Suppressing and Dissolving the Ego

Commentary on Chapter 10   **171**
Yin and Yang

Commentary on Chapter 11   **173**
Rationalizing the Pursuit of Power; Importance of Our Spiritual Network

Commentary on Chapter 12   **177**
Not Manipulating Others; Being Open to the Deeper Lesson

Commentary on Chapter 13   **179**
Psychic Shields; Thoughts from the outside; Dark Tractor Beams; Implications of Awakening; Importance of Developing Discernment through Meditation; Brains as Transmitters and Receivers; Co-Creating Reality and Inter-dependent Vortexes

Commentary on Chapter 14   **185**
Parallels between Spiritual Teachers and Role Models in Business and other Parts of Our Lives

Commentary on Chapter 15   **189**
Tibetan Buddhism and Absolute vs. Full Enlightenment

Commentary on Chapter 16   **195**
Multiple Thought Seeds—Unaligned Manifestation as Black Magic; Forgiveness; Bliss; Channeling; Resistance and Acceptance; Other Topics

Commentary on Chapter 17   **199**
Drugs, Sex and Hidden Addictions; Craving
Center Co-opting our Spiritual Paths and
those of our Teachers; Healing Wounds and
Clearing Karma through Directed
Compassion—Practical Application;
Being Mindful of our Intentions and
How We Use Information and Power

Epilogue   **209**

Introduction

THE MOST IMPORTANT thing you could possibly do right now is to consciously and powerfully surrender to Divine Will, your Highest Self, your Most Fully Conscious and Enlightened Self, or whatever other label you ascribe to what I am referring to. In this surrender process it is recommended that you ask God and/or the Universe and/or your Highest Self for ever-increasing discernment and faith.

All spiritual teachings, religious traditions and our own personal experiences eventually lead us to this place, to this simple formula.

If you have never surrendered in this way and asked for ever-increasing discernment and faith, I recommend that you do so right now. If you have already done it, I recommend that you do so right now. If you have already done it a thousand times, I recommend that you do so right now.

The path of enlightenment is the path of surrendering ever more deeply to Divine Will, our Highest Self, our Most Fully Conscious and Enlightened Self, or whatever other label you ascribe to what I am referring to. There is no other way.

And while this may sound like a simple task, there are a number of pitfalls that an earnest spiritual seeker can accidentally fall into along this passageway – on the way to completely realizing and continuously embodying their Most Fully Conscious and Enlightened Self. The aim of this book is to highlight some of the most common and/or dangerous traps that people encounter during their search for Freedom and Truth, and to outline a new map of the spiritual path and Reality As It Is, which is far more accurate than those in common use today, i.e., a greatly improved map that will support spiritual seekers in more effectively navigating life and reality in order to reach their worthy goals.

A major reason so many of us have inaccurate maps of reality, flawed mental models and belief systems, is that we perceive the small slice of reality that we do actually perceive, through a lens which is often not clear and which is warped in various areas to various degrees. As such, during our search for Truth, we can be exposed to the purest form of light, the most profound and simplest and purest spiritual teaching, and when that light comes through our lens, it will be distorted and we will be unable to receive it in its pure state. In assimilating these teachings, we bend and distort them, we misinterpret or misunderstand them, and in our thoughts, speech and actions in living our day to day lives, we misapply them with sometimes profoundly negative consequences. The Truth can be right in front of us, but we can't see or experience it because our lens is too cloudy, too warped and with too many fractures and cracks. An important part of our emotional, spiritual and intellectual development then, is to fix, clean and straighten out our lens, and in some cases learn to have experiences where we can get around our lens entirely in order to have direct experience of Reality As It Is.

There is a parable I heard once about a devil in training under the tutelage of a more senior devil. One day the person to whom they are assigned (their "assignment") stumbles across a rare and unique book containing pure Truth. The more junior devil is alarmed because he does not want this person to move out of confusion into the Light of Truth, so he starts running ideas past the senior devil regarding how they can separate their assignment from this book of Truth. Maybe they can have him get in a car accident and the book will be destroyed. Maybe they can have him put it in his bag carelessly so it falls out and he loses it. Maybe they can arrange for his bag to be stolen and for the person who steals the bag to throw the book away, not realizing what it is and thinking that it has no value. After the senior devil listens to all of these ideas, he laughs at the more junior devil. He says, "Haha, my young and idiotic fool. Our assignment finding this book is good for us. We don't have to separate him from this book. We will interpret it for him."

Of course, more often than not, our challenges are compounded by the fact we are not carrying around the book of Truth, but instead we are carrying around books of partial truths, half truths, unintentional distortions of the Truth, or books with a few morsels of pure Truth and Light surrounded by clumps of confusion and often times well-meaning suggestions to follow dead end paths. And, these are the good spiritual books I am referring to! The bad ones are written by people who are wittingly or unwittingly acting as channels for darkness to come through under the false pretense of light. The consciousness intending the deception may not be that of the channel, the author being used as a vehicle in this way.

In our quest for Truth and Enlightenment, we must at times rely on well-meaning yet imperfect teachers, while doing our best to avoid dark teachers and false prophets. There are more of the latter group out there than most of us realize or would want to admit. Sometimes seeing Reality As It Is can be disheartening, which is why we shield our self from seeing it to begin with. Our mind protects us from aspects of reality that cause us pain or in some cases that our nervous system simply isn't able to process yet. This built in protection mechanism – i.e., coping mechanism – often serves an important and positive purpose but at the cost of keeping us in delusion until we make the conscious and sometimes long term efforts necessary to develop the emotional, mental and physiological capacity to move out of untruth into the Light of Truth.

Every crack and warping in our perceptual lens maps to an emotional or physical trauma that we have experienced in this life or in lifetimes past, or that has been passed to us through family or other important ties. Every pathological or distorted thought form in our mind keeping us in confusion has corresponding aspects in our emotional and energetic bodies. Fixing our perceptual lens, straightening out our warped mind, requires resolution on other levels, not just the mental level. At the same time, sometimes coming into emotional alignment first requires a new mental model, a new way to intellectually frame and understand certain situations or events. There is no primacy of spirit over matter, energy over body, or emotions over mind. All of these things are interdependent and form the complex matrix of Reality As It Is, including our mind-body system.

This book primarily works at the level of mind. Not because of primacy of mind, but because this is what I was moved to write about, and because getting things right at the level of our mental map and belief systems is a critical part of our awakening process, a critical step leading us toward greater joy, happiness and abundance… and Enlightenment. Unfortunately, most of our minds are at least partially full of confusion; cluttered with half-truths, distortions of the truth, or blatant lies; infected by unhealthy mental viruses and pathological thought patterns; and in some cases completely dominated by addictions or external agents of which we are sometimes not even aware.

We have much work to do.

My intention in writing this book is to help all sentient beings take important and powerful steps forward, out of confusion and into the Light of Truth. Many of the mental traps outlined in this book are ones I have fallen into myself during the more than 20 years I have been on a conscious path of personal development and spiritual growth. Others I have been fortunate to avoid and are simply those I see others getting caught in on a regular basis. Some of these unintended snares are hidden in the writings of well-known authors and teachers like Deepak Chopra, one of the most influential authors in my life for several years, and a well-meaning, highly realized spiritual teacher. Others are found in traditional Buddhist teachings, in popular books such as The Secret, or in the writings of one of the world's current favorites, Eckhart Tolle. It is debatable whether any teacher is a pure vessel, and in any case, even if we come across a pure vessel it does not mean that our warped minds can receive their pure light in its fullness and clarity. Traps are everywhere, including in commonly held cultural beliefs like the notion of a silver lining, the topic of the book's first chapter.

Not that I want to sound at all discouraging. The good news is that once we are aware of specific pitfalls we can avoid falling into them, or we can catch our self when falling in and get out more quickly. Like a golfer or a sharp shooter who is aware of the direction and speed of the wind, once we become aware of the distortions in our own perceptual lens we can make adjustments to compensate so that we are better able to hit our targets in life. Such compensation is a good tool we can use until we can complete the deeper and often lengthier process of actually fixing the lens. Further, the good news is that once we become intimately involved with identifying, compensating for and eventually transforming some number of perceptual distortions and their accompanying emotional wounds helping anchor them into us, we can develop an increasing capacity to perform these tasks more effectively and efficiently in the future. We can more quickly identify and cure our own blind spots, our own mental diseases, and we can be a better mirror and more supportive and compassionate friend for other seekers yearning for the joy and peace of the Clear Light.

There IS a light at the end of the tunnel, and we don't even have to grasp at it or yearn for it, in order for it to overtake us. At some point in the process, we will have accomplished enough for our full immersion in light to become inevitable. Which means, in fact, that this full immersion is already inevitable.

You may question the validity of this assertion right now, but hopefully, by the time you finish reading this book, you will know at a very deep level that what I am saying here is 100% true with no room for doubt or debate. Conscious or unconscious, willing or unwilling, we are all on this path. It is the fundamental nature of consciousness and all of life to make this journey—the journey to full enlightenment—whether we are willing or aware of this at any point in time.

Take a deep breathe. Even as new challenges lie ahead, somewhere else you have already overcome them.

I have written this book in two sections in order to accommodate two different voices, styles of communication and types of content. It is roughly modeled on any number of Buddhist books that incorporate a root text of older origins with commentary from a current teacher. In this specific instance, the commentary in Part II affords us the opportunity to explore in a less sequential and structured fashion some important topics that build on and/ or reinforce multiple aspects of the foundational material introduced in Part I. As such, while some of the topics in the second section outlined in the table of contents might sound interesting and tempt you to skip ahead, I recommend that you read Part I in its entirety before reading Part II, and that generally speaking you read the book in the order in which I have presented it. Also, with regards to Buddhism, you will note that this is not a Buddhist text, and that, in fact, there is much Truth presented in this book that calls into question or directly contradicts a number of Buddhist teachings. I have simply borrowed a convention often found in Buddhist writings as the basic format of this volume.

Furthermore, as it relates to the book's structure, I want to highlight the relevance of the endnotes. They are not afterthoughts, and in many cases they contain important information that can be central to the thought processes spurred by what I write. There are a couple instances in particular that if you apply what I have written in the text without reading the endnotes, you may later regret doing so. I believe they are all worthwhile, of course, and perhaps the ones that are most important are: 18, 24, 26, and 29.

A meaningful portion of mainstream thinking in the modern spiritual community has gotten pretty far off target, leading to a great deal of unnecessary suffering for many earnest seekers. And, of course, the same is true in more formal religious contexts, as well. In the West and around the world, many spiritual teachers and teachings – old and new – are leading millions of heartfelt individuals in the wrong direction, away from Truth and happiness, or perhaps in some cases, leading them generally in the right direction but not pointing out important pitfalls, which, if fallen into, can result in lengthy, painful delays. I have written this book with the hope that it will accelerate your process of enlightenment and save you needless years, decades or lifetimes spent stuck in a trap or following roads to nowhere. I hope that in my writings and in my life, I can do my small part to help as many people who are willing and able to adjust course where needed and take steps that are sure and true, ones that lead them towards the achievement of their positive goals. I hope you will find this book thought-provoking, challenging and rewarding, and that it will serve as a useful instrument in your efforts to cut yourself free from confusion en route to achieving Freedom and Enlightenment.

Thank you for reading <u>Reinventing Truth</u>, and thank you for achieving Freedom and Enlightenment. Namaste.

Part I

chapter 1.

THINGS WENT WRONG. Don't be fooled by the silver lining.

When things in our lives go badly, it can be extremely painful. Losing a job, a loved one. Making a terrible choice that impacts our lives for years or decades in profoundly unpleasant ways that no matter how hard we try it seems impossible to overcome and recover from. Being victimized in some way—sexually abused as a child, slandered at work or in the community, convicted of a crime we did not commit.

When faced with intense emotional pain, our brain responds with several types of coping mechanisms. Coping mechanisms are a 100% healthy psychological response that our brain utilizes to protect us from psychological pain that is too much to handle and from layers of reality that we are not yet ready to deal with. Part of the genius of our mind is an innate knowledge regarding just how much reality our system can take and making sure we don't get any more than we can constructively process. Coping mechanisms keep us from killing our self, going insane, or otherwise having a total system meltdown that would be harmful and not serve us. Somehow, there is a great intelligence within us that knows when the truth would be harmful and that protects us via various forms of self-deluding. This intelligence knows that at this specific time at this specific stage of our development, the lesser evil is to shroud the truth… for now… until the right time in the future when it's OK for us to see it.

One of the most common coping mechanisms that we use and which has been passed down from generation to generation is the concept of the silver lining.

Two Case Studies

Several months ago I began facilitating individuals in working through and transforming issues confronting them in their emotional and spiritual life. I had picked up a lot of tools and techniques working with various "healers"[1] and healing modalities for over a decade, and more recently I began having pretty significant shifts in my perception of reality and my understanding of the process of healing and transformation that we humans go through on the path towards Enlightenment and the experience of Completion. I was in an elongated transition in my own life exploring different aspects of myself, and given how much benefit I had received from working with various healers and the likes over the years, I thought it would be both fulfilling and interesting to help others in their processes of growth and transformation, while simultaneously investigating the extent of my abilities in this arena. In a period of roughly 6 months, I worked with some 20+ "clients" on a pro-bono or barter basis, offering to help them with whatever might be troubling them. As fate would have it[2], just as I was writing this chapter, I worked with two different clients whose situations and attitudes illustrate some of the points I want to communicate herein.

One of these clients was a man we will call Jason. Jason is a relatively young man in his early thirties, and at the time of our session his mother was going in for surgery and her health was generally on the decline. Both Jason and his mother believed her days may be numbered. During our phone call we discovered that he subconsciously wanted his mother to die. She and his father had been pretty terrible to him during his childhood—using various forms of emotional abuse and psychological manipulation, intentionally breaking him down and making him think he was crazy, and doing things that he experienced as torture. Things were so bad for him, that as a teenager he would cut himself, and he came very close to attempting suicide. While exploring these issues over the phone together, he made the offhand remark that he was thankful his parents were so terrible and unsupportive. It was this lack of support at home that led him to seek out support elsewhere and which eventually led him to find his current spiritual faith and spiritual teachers—teachers he greatly loves and admires and who have helped him make tremendous strides on many levels.

In another recent session with a woman we will call Janie, we were working through some difficult issues she is currently facing in her career in which for a number of reasons she has been unable to reach as wide of an audience as she would like with important truths that have been revealed to her and that could help many, many people if she were able to get her message out more broadly. As part of her process we spent some time working with several of her early childhood memories. Hers was a childhood in which there had been all manner of strangeness and difficulty, very hard things for a young girl to deal with—her mother disappearing without explanation, having to raise the younger kids on her own from the age of nine, a troubled father who created very difficult and emotionally trying situations for her, living in poverty and the likes. While recounting a myriad of facts that painted a pretty rough picture, she mentioned off-hand that this unusually difficult childhood had made her strong. Janie is in her sixties and said this in a tone of voice typical I believe of many people from her generation, whereas she felt as if she caught herself complaining about her tough childhood and realized it's not an acceptable thing to do, that she must be tough and look at the bright side of even the darkest of situations. That somehow things weren't so bad after all, not as bad as other peoples' lives or as bad as things could have been, so she should look at the bright side and somehow this makes everything OK. Her tough childhood did make her strong after all. Right?

    Thoughts like the ones Jason and Janie expressed during their sessions are coping mechanisms that served them well for many years but which do not serve them anymore. In identifying the silver lining, these individuals were able to tell themselves that these bad things happened for a reason, that they were part of some plan for their lives, that they ultimately brought some benefit along with the pain and suffering, and in that, because of the silver lining, the pain and suffering were at least bearable, perhaps worth it. Maybe they were even able to convince themselves that their misfortune was really a blessing in disguise. If as children or young adults they had realized that none of this hardship brought them even one ounce of goodness, this stark reality might have been too much to bear, it may have pushed them into places too dark for them to deal with, places that may have lead them to very unfortunate behaviors or to deeper negative feelings that they were not yet able or ready to breathe through and process. It is a good thing they developed these coping mechanisms to shield them from seeing Reality As It Is, from feeling the full pain of realizing what they lost, what was unjustly taken from them without any compensation, from seeing a reality that would have been too painful for them to deal with back then at a time when they did not have the support or tools to deal with such difficult things.

In both these cases however, the silver linings are in fact misattributions, self-deluding, and a lack of understanding of causation.

How Silver Linings Hurt Us

This type of thinking – focusing on the silver lining and not realizing that things just went wrong – is greatly limiting and can be damaging in a number of ways.

First, if every time something bad happens we try to see the good in it, we run the risk of subconsciously attracting more bad things into our life. We run the risk of confusing our self and thinking that bad things are actually good things. If we program our self into thinking painful, traumatic experiences have all sorts of benefits (or are a necessary part of our process of spiritual growth and development), we are very likely going to find our self having more painful, traumatic experiences.

Second, on some level our system knows that we are lying to our self with these rationalizations. Lying to our self takes quite a bit of energy. Our body knows that something bad happened, but our mind is telling us that it was actually a good thing and part of the Divine Plan for our life or some such nonsense. We are in conflict with our self and in denial of reality. Once we accept in our mind what our body already knows, we can feel the release of the tension, the uncoiling of the inner conflict and the liberation that comes from moving out of denial and into acceptance of reality. Our whole system – physical, emotional, mental and energetic – functions better and more smoothly. This can free up a tremendous amount of energy that we can redirect towards creating the life we want for our self and achieving greater levels of joy, abundance and enlightenment. As we move out of denial more and more, we will become more physically healthy and vibrant, and we will develop greater mental and emotional capacity to deal with Reality As It Is, with less need for coping mechanisms in the future.

Third, it is incredibly difficult to give our self compassion for something bad that happened if we cannot accept that it was in fact bad, if we are too focused on the silver lining and in denial of how painful reality truly was and is. Compassion is the single most powerful healing force on the planet, and until we are able to see reality for what it is, accept that something went wrong in our life, we will be largely deprived of this powerful healing energy. Not only will we be unable to give our self compassion, it will be less likely that others will give us compassion or that we will be able to accept their compassion if they offer it.

Finally, if we become overly accustomed to seeing the silver lining in any situation, then when we find our self in confusing or difficult circumstances in life, we will be less likely to make the significant effort necessary to discern for our self what is actually best for us. AND, even if we are able to dig deeply to see what is best, we will then be less likely to go to the great lengths that are often necessary in order to follow the proper course and achieve the outcome we know to be right. We will pre-emptively rationalize and accept the lesser result and more often take the path of least resistance, even in those cases when it is the wrong path. Our convictions will be weakened, and we will become more passive in our approach to creating the joyful life we are truly meant to live. Because we trust that whatever happens will be for the best and that "everything happens for a reason", we will just let things happen – even when we shouldn't – and we will end up becoming overly accepting of an existence that is far less than what is actually possible for us.

Pulling Away the Silver Linings

Now that you are aware of a number of their negative consequences, perhaps you are ready to pull away some of the silver linings in your life and face the tough reality that some things just went wrong – no ifs, ands, or buts about it. Some time you may want to make a list of all the things that went wrong with your life and all the silver linings you have used in the past to convince yourself that these painful turns in life weren't so bad after all. Maybe now is a good time to do this.

Some of these silver linings can be very compelling, but don't be fooled. Really think about how if that bad thing hadn't happened, how things would have been different. Would you still have a livelihood? Friends? A spouse and kids? Could you have possibly met some of the same people a different way if they were really meant to be in your life? How would you have been different as a person and who would be your closest friends instead if they weren't the same people? Would they also be people you love and care about and people who love and care about you? Is it possible they would be people on a higher vibration, pulling you further up in life and bringing more joy and goodness into your life even than the friends you have now? Could you have gained some of the same wisdom and insight in a more pleasurable way? Or even greater wisdom and insight through a more favorable sequence of events and outcomes?

You may be having difficulty seeing that you could have been as well off or even better off than you are now, that you could have had all the good things you have in your life—or better things—without having gone through all the pain and suffering, as well. You might be thinking had that terrible thing in your past gone differently, gone in a better way, that other good things since might have also gone differently, gone in a worse direction. Maybe you wouldn't have that good job, maybe you would have had a spouse you don't love as much, maybe you would have had a miscarriage or given birth to a severely handicapped child, maybe even you would have gotten into a car accident and been paralyzed or killed. It is easy for us to imagine all sorts of misfortune, all sorts of tragedy, all manner by which our lives could have turned out worse. Maybe you hear thoughts running through your head like,

It's best we don't even think about these things. We should just be thankful for what we have, thankful that the bad things in our life have led to good things, and thankful that things didn't go worse, that things are as good as they are.

But please, let us stop and ponder for a moment. What is the limiting belief behind this thought pattern? Where is your thinking flawed?

First, you might immediately see that you hold the limiting belief that things in your life fundamentally can't be any better than they are. It's as if there is a thermostat setting regarding the quality of your life and that the balance of good and bad is relatively fixed. If something bad happens that brings your overall quality of life below a certain threshold, then magically some number of good things will happen to bring it back into the set range; and conversely, if some number of good things happen to bring your quality of life above the set range, then watch out, bad things are coming to bring your life back into alignment with the thermostat setting. If this is true for you, if you hold this subconscious belief, then at some level you probably don't think you deserve or are worthy of a better life.

Second, you might see a deeper and more subtle type of flawed thinking, which is a general confusion about causation. Typically, most people see causation based on linear time and based on a Newtonian view of the world.

Something bad happened and afterward something good happened in a way that looks related via the circumstances that this bad thing apparently created. It must be then that the bad thing caused the good thing. It's like two billiard balls on a pool table. The cue ball hits the red ball at a certain angle, so the red ball goes into the pocket—Newtonian causation in linear time. And, while on one level of reality many things in this physical world we live in follow Newtonian physics and mechanistic patterns, none of the most important things in our lives are governed by these rules. Love, death, health and illness, accidents, financial well-being, that promotion or new job, positive relationships with friends and family, that new person that shows up unexpectedly at just the right moment in your life when you really need them – all of these things, all of the greatest determinants of human health and happiness, all of these are governed by different forces, all of these take place based on a different cosmology within a universe that is different than the Newtonian one that most people see in their day to day existence. In order to really understand causation and see through the delusion of the silver lining, we must embrace a different way of seeing things, a different world-view.

Introduction to Metaphysics and Metaphysical Causation

The higher and more basic truth in this instance is that our souls are constantly projecting our self into this physical reality and are constantly taking part in coordinating all manner of events and situations in our lives so that we can see the reflection of our inner reality, the reflection of the state of our souls, in the mirror of the physical world

Reinventing Truth

around us. Perhaps you are already very familiar with The Law of Attraction, or most likely you have at least heard something like "We create our own reality. Our outer world reflects our inner world." There is a great amount of truth in this statement, and what we are talking about here is the very real reality of metaphysical causation[3].

Perhaps you have heard the explanation before about the movie projector? It's as if the physical reality we are living in is a movie being projected onto a screen, and we are the main character in the movie. As a character in the movie in ordinary awareness we are not even aware that the projector exists and is projecting light through a film imprinted with images in order to create the movie, creating us and our world. We are completely engrossed in the drama, and in that drama all the events are unfolding based on the rules of normal physical reality such as Newtonian physics and linear causation in time. What we are missing is that nothing that happens in the movie causes anything else in the movie, even though that's what it looks like from within the movie. Everything is actually caused by the projector. It is the hidden cause. One character shooting another character does not cause the second character's death. The movie projector and what is imprinted on the film that the light is shining through is actually what is causing everything. In this analogy our souls are the movie projector, the images on the film are the imprints on our souls, and the life we are living in physical reality is the movie. It is important to point out here that your soul is not just projecting you into physical reality, it is projecting the entire movie that is your whole life—attracting all of the people, situations and events that you encounter in this drama in the physical realm. This movie analogy used to explain the metaphysical worldview is in fact a simplification of important aspects of The True Nature of Reality, aspects of Reality that a number of religious texts and spiritual teachers have been trying to convey to us with mixed success for hundreds and thousands of years.

So in this reality, if we are fully enlightened, if our souls are a pure ball of light with no wounds or obscurations at the soul level, if we are completely healed and whole, then our lives are an unending sequence of increasingly positive and joyful events and circumstances. No wounds means no negative imprints on the soul[4], on the film. Our inner perfection is reflected/projected outwards into a perfect life in the outer world, constantly providing us with positive feedback regarding the perfection of our inner state of being[5].

Most of us, however, have not reached that point in our journey. Our souls are still wounded. We have not yet realized our true nature of being totally healed and whole. We have obscurations and are not yet fully enlightened. There are some negative imprints on the film of our soul. As such, our soul draws forth people and situations into our reality that help us experience both where we are healthy and where we are wounded. The "bad" things or difficult things reflect our wounds and blocks, and they provide us with negative feedback so we can see where the inner condition of our soul is less than 100% healthy and clear, so we can see where we need to shine the light of our loving heart, where we need to heal our self. These are the bad scenes in the movie.

Applying Metaphysics to See through the Illusion of the Silver Lining

Returning to our original topic of silver linings, if you can take on this viewpoint for a moment, you can see then that bad things don't cause good things. This never happens and in fact cannot ever happen. Your soul, the projector, causes all things in your life[6]. Light, i.e., healthy parts of your soul, causes good things. Wounds and potholes on your soul cause bad things. There is no such thing as a silver lining! Plain and simple. So, when a bad thing is followed by a good thing in this drama of life, the proverbial silver lining, it is not that there is any causation between these things whatsoever. It is instead our souls projecting both the light and dark into physical reality—the single hidden cause behind both the good and the bad—and our souls are showing us "Here is where you need to heal, but don't worry, here are some other places where things are already healthy and whole, where your light is shining through clearly."

Since seeing the silver lining is such an incredibly common and old mental habit for so many people, such a powerful habit in the collective mind stream—even if part of you can see that what I am saying here is a more accurate way of seeing reality, you still may be having some difficulty letting go of this old way of perceiving things, right now, in real time, as you are reading this book. That's OK. Hopefully at least, we have opened a new doorway and helped you catch a glimpse of this new world view for the time being, and you will experience and live into metaphysical reality more and more deeply over time.

Integrating Lost Parts of Your Soul by Dropping the Silver Lining and Moving into Reality As It Is

When you move more deeply into the paradigm of metaphysical causation, and when you are able to drop out of the illusion that things in your life had to go the way they did and that you are better off as a result—when you are able to do this—you may find that a positive and beneficial process can and will begin to unfold in your life. If you can look at just one painful event in your life, one bad thing, and you are able to accept that it was bad and did not account for even one ounce of goodness in your life, then you will be able to truly give yourself compassion for this bad thing, and furthermore, you will feel safe imagining how things might have unfolded differently and in a better way. You may be able to imagine this different life path right now in several minutes or perhaps different bits and pieces of this alternate reality will come through and occur to you over the course of several hours, days or weeks. The more you allow your imagination to go into this parallel life, the more that will be revealed to you—possibilities you never imagined, insights regarding the unfolding of your life. And, with each new bit that comes through you may have little "aha" moments and feel endorphins released in your mind and in your body.

Somewhere along the way you might feel very sad, realizing that things really could have gone differently—you really could have had a better life—and in that moment, you can mourn the loss of this better life that should have been. And, as you work through these steps, at some point in the process of going more deeply into your parallel life that should have been, you may start to have an energetic experience and feel inside yourself as if you actually lived this alternative life. It's like somehow the strength and happiness and peace and joy and fulfillment of this parallel you is merging into your body and into your energy field. You get the benefit as if things had gone the right way. You feel peace and warmth in your body, in your abdomen. You feel a sense of relief, experience a full-body sigh of relief, and you hear a voice say,

Things worked out well, the way I wanted them to, the way they were supposed to.

In that moment, that parallel you gets fully integrated into current you. You are reunited with a part of your soul that was taken away when things went wrong, and this is a very, very good thing.

Two Case Studies Revisited

I told Jason that he could have had a supportive, positive family life AND found his faith and spiritual teachers, that he could have had an unbroken chain of support—supportive parents followed by supportive spiritual teachers. I explained to him that he had misunderstood causation in this situation to cope with a difficult part of reality he was not ready to see yet. He is someone I had worked with a number of times before, someone I knew could deal with a direct approach. We worked through this aspect of the session until he got it, until he could see through the illusion of the silver lining, and then we were able to continue to move forward in the larger process and arrive at a place where he no longer wanted his mother to die, a place where he could see clearly what he really wanted for his mom and their relationship, desires that had been buried beneath layers of disillusion and despair and anger and other difficult feelings. He got to a place by the end of the call where he felt he could start to be somewhat supportive—directly or indirectly—in her recovery process.

I told Janie that she might have been strong anyway (implying that her difficult childhood experiences may not have been necessary or the cause of her strength), to which she only responded with a thoughtful "Hmm?", the sound someone makes when a new idea strikes them as a possibility that they had never considered before. This was our first session together, and it did not feel important to address this issue head on, only to suggest the possibility that the silver lining was not real but a coping mechanism. And this was only a small, somewhat tangential point to the bigger picture we were dealing with anyway. By the end of this session she had made a great deal of progress giving herself compassion for past difficulties and dissolving out a good chunk of the karmic pattern we were working on, and by the end of our second session later the same week, she had completely dissolved out the karmic wound and pattern that had been burdening her for at least three lifetimes she is aware of (including this one). As a result, near the end of our second session, she had a fairly profound experience of re-writing her past and living into the parallel reality she always knew was right. And, in reliving specific experiences in the new and positive way, she was able to feel this other reality in her cells and in her body, making a new imprint all the way in at the soul level. Because of this experience of rewriting and re-living the past, going forward in her life things can unfold according to the new imprint. We rewrote the script/shifted the pattern, and now her life will naturally unfold in a positive way, following the new pattern of things going right. Provided there aren't any other big karmic blocks, other big wounds in this area of her life that haven't surfaced yet, her soul can project into physical reality situations and events that let her see herself as healed and whole, not wounded anymore.

In both of these cases the silver lining coping mechanism was present but not central to these individuals' processes, and in both cases they were able to transform as much of their issues that they needed to at this point in time—one of them entirely and the other enough to create an opening for new possibilities in his relationship with his mother. And while pulling back the silver lining was not central, it was an important aspect of their work.

Final Thoughts on Silver Linings

It is impossible to fully heal a wound when we are holding onto its perceived benefits. It is impossible to fully dissolve an obscuration, fully transform a pattern when we ascribe benefit to its past fruition and unknowingly ascribe benefit to it playing out again in the future. Seeing through the false reality of the silver lining is extremely important and beneficial, and it is something far too few people have done up until now. The fact that you are reading these words right now means that you are ready to pull back many of the silver linings in your life and enjoy the benefits of moving more deeply into Reality As It Really Is, not as we want or need it to be. Congratulations for getting to this point in your process. Good things are coming your way faster and faster now.

chapter 2.

JUST LIKE SOMETIMES things went wrong, many "bad" things are actually bad.

Earlier today when I was thinking of writing this book, I was feeling a little bit of embarrassment, looking at myself through the eyes of "normal" mainstream people who are not on a spiritual path. Pretty much the whole world knows that bad things are bad. But, somehow, I am part of this minority group that considers themselves to be on some sort of spiritual path, and now someone needs to write a book to explain to them that bad things are actually bad?

It's like somehow when we are exposed to new truths and new realities that bring us great joy and insight and growth, it seems we are prone to forgetting common sense. This is because many of these new insights and truths are exciting and represent breakthroughs because of the fact they overturn our old beliefs. Our old beliefs brought us a lot of pain and suffering, and limited our joy and expansiveness. We were happy to let those old beliefs die with our old pain body, but the problem is those old beliefs might not have been all false. We might sometimes throw the baby out with the bathwater. We might sometimes overcompensate. We get so caught up in our shiny new toy, this new belief system, it overtakes us and seems like all there is; its shininess crowds out the rest of our field of vision. These new truths are so exciting they seem like the whole truth. The Truth is, they are not. And this points us towards some of the most nuanced but important challenges we face on our spiritual path. How do we integrate new truths without losing the benefit of the old truths? How do we simultaneously occupy multiple layers of reality that seem contradictory? How do we know when to apply which layer of truth and move seamlessly between the spiritual, metaphysical, physical, relative, absolute, subjective, objective, emotional, and rational aspects of reality? Can we stretch our mind and experience all of these at the same time?

There is a great benefit in being able to withhold judgment about apparently "bad" things. Perhaps if we have a more positive attitude, this apparently "bad" thing will turn into a good thing and lead to good outcomes. It is not what happens to us in life, but how we respond to it. If we unconsciously react instead of consciously respond, our reaction to an apparently "bad" thing can lead to bigger and badder things, and we might find our self on the negative end of a self-fulfilling prophecy. All of this is true, and developing the ability to withhold judgment, maintain a positive attitude, and respond instead of react are certainly good and useful things to do.

Furthermore, developing the ability to go into a deeply peaceful meditation and into a transcendent spiritual reality where you can accept bad things and be at total peace

Reinventing Truth

with the unfolding of your life and the universe exactly as it is taking place—this is also a good thing to do. It is great if you can get to a place where you can sit in non-judgment with total peace in your body and in your breathe as you hold in your awareness the aspects of humanity and your life that bring up the strongest and most difficult feelings for you—whether it be human rights abuses, genocide and slavery; environmental destruction and animal cruelty; or discrimination based on gender or sexual preference—or whether it is something awful that happened to you or someone you love. There is much wisdom and benefit to be gained from attaining these transcended states of consciousness, practicing non-judgment, and seeing and experiencing the world from a non-ordinary perspective.

And even though we live in a spiritual and metaphysical world, we also live in a physical world. Much of life is ordinary, and it is useful to be able to live and function in ordinary consciousness. Perhaps you have heard of the expression, "First enlightenment. Then the laundry." The point of enlightenment or spiritual transcendence or seeing the world from non-ordinary states of consciousness or points of view is not to live in this alternate reality 24 hours a day for the rest of our lives and avoid all the pain of normal reality and regular physical existence. If you are after true mastery, then what you want to do is to develop full range of motion in your consciousness. You want to be completely free to experience the tremendous flexibility inherent in our human consciousness and not be attached to staying in any one place forever or for even for more than one second, even if it's the most beautiful, joyful, blissful place and state of being you have ever experienced or believe you ever will. The point of all of this is to develop the ability to be, and to actually be, totally and 100% aligned with the intelligence of the universe, with God[7], with Divine Will, with your Highest Good—and to follow that wherever it takes you. Sometimes, Divine Will for your life may be to be in a transcendent reality at peace with all the "bad" things going on around you, feeling blissed out knowing that all is well and as it should be. Other times, Divine Will for your life might be for you to be down in the trenches in the physical world and in a "less enlightened" place, seeing that the bad things are bad, and taking action fueled by your anger at the injustice you see around you, battling for good, right here, right now, with your bare feet and your hands in the dirt.

chapter 3.

ONE OF THE most important implications of the metaphysical reality outlined in Chapter 1 is that we are empowered creators of our own reality, and as such, we are not victims, and there are no victims at all. At the same time, it is also true that there are victims and you have probably been victimized in your life.

As suggested in the last chapter, it is important as we grow in our spiritual maturity that we stop moving from one partial truth to another partial truth and thinking we have finally "gotten it", moving from being lost in one side of the paradox to being lost in the other side of the paradox, the side we hadn't understood before. It is time now to take it to the next level, to become highly realized beings with discriminating wisdom and an expanded and more accurate experience of reality. You need this for yourself now, and the world needs this from you too.

If you have not already done so, reconciling the victim paradox is one of the most important steps you can take towards total healing and becoming a more empowered and compassionate actor in your own life and as a global citizen, making your life and the world at large a better and more joyful place.

Many times near the beginning of our spiritual awakening, we have trouble accepting the metaphysical truth that we are not victims and that there are no victims at all. We can't help but think of all the times bad things have happened to us and those we love, and seeing so many victims of terrible things around us in the world today and throughout history. But, as our experience of soul-identification increases over time, we are able to see with increasingly clarity that our soul chose to be born into this physical body, this life, and to learn these lessons. And, in learning metaphysics and going more deeply into the experience of metaphysical reality, we are able to see with increasingly clarity that we have attracted the people and situations into our life that are happening all the time. If we were stolen from or attacked or violated or lied to and used; if we were diagnosed with cancer or another painful or life threatening illness; or if we were hit by a car or injured in a natural disaster (things that are clearly outside of our control!)—we understand that it is useful to see that we are not a victim. It is empowering, even though sometimes very difficult, to shift out of our ordinary perspective, (i.e., our current ego perspective and seeing the world from the vantage point of "the little me"), and to identify with our soul—to see and experience just how powerful our soul really is, and to take on the level of self-responsibility that is the necessary consequence of having these realizations. Many people would prefer to be a victim than to be self-responsible, so they never get over this extremely important hurdle and never take one of the most powerful steps forward towards heal-

Reinventing Truth

ing and spiritual growth. For those of us who do make it over this first hurdle, it is incredibly empowering to see and experience that we—at the level of our soul—are 100% and fully responsible for our experiences here in these bodies; that our outer world is a perfect reflection of our inner world, which means that we can change our outer world at any point in time by turning inward and with our own loving compassion, healing whatever wounds might be reflecting outwards onto the movie screen of our life. Once we know and experience this truth in our mind and in our body and in our day-to-day experience of reality, we know then at a very deep level that we can re-create our life consciously. We know at a very deep level that we can heal our self physically and emotionally, create a better life for our self and our loved ones, and do our part in supporting the healing of others and the world around us. As we continue to progress, at some point in our journey, we have the wonderful realization that everything does, in fact, happen for a reason, and that reason is to support all of us fully knowing our Self and True Nature, to support our process of unfolding into a pure light being, experiencing the bliss of full enlightenment[8]. As our soul identification strengthens and this realization deepens, we become increasingly empowered, and we see with increasing clarity that we are not a victim, we never were a victim and there are not now nor have there ever been any victims at all. We see that we are and always have been at cause in our life, and we are excited at the wonderful implications of all of this, excited about what this means for us, for the people we love and for all of humanity. From this vantage point, we feel compassion for those that are caught in the illusion of victim hood, and we want to do whatever we can to help them wake up and leave behind that incredibly painful, limiting and dis-empowering experience of reality.

While all of this is very positive, many people who reach this point in their journey fall into the trap of believing that their new vantage point, their new, "more enlightened" perspective on reality, is a correct and complete perception of Reality As It Is. Many people who get this far are so thrilled with the benefits of their new truth, they go from being lost in one side of the paradox to being lost in the other side of the paradox. They miss the broader Truth, which is, once we break out of victim mentality, it is actually safe for us to acknowledge and deal with the times in our life when we have been victimized. I realize this may be a little confusing. While there are many benefits in moving out of victim mentality, there are problems that arise from living in a victimless world. The idea is not to regress back into victim hood or to some midway compromise viewpoint, but to progress forward into embracing paradox and simultaneously occupying two seemingly contradictory layers of reality.

So, while it is real in metaphysical reality (i.e., at the level of soul identification) that we are not now and never have been a victim, it is also real that in the physical world (i.e., at the level of typical ego identification) we have probably been victimized, and this is particularly true regarding bad things that might have happened to us when we were a child. If we were an abused child, we were a victim—on one level. While it can be healing and empowering to embrace the spiritual/metaphysical reality, if we only embrace this level of reality we are in denial of another layer of reality. If just for a moment we can put to the side past

Reinventing Truth

lives and karma and our soul choosing this life; if just for a moment we can put aside the metaphysical truth that our outer world reflects our inner world and hence we are fully responsible for both of these worlds… if we can put these things aside for a moment, we can remember that this little boy or little girl was beaten by their parents. They were confused and scared. They were emotionally and physically dependent on these parents and not in a position to fight back or leave to fend for them self. This vulnerable child was defenseless and powerless. This child was a victim.

After we take a step forward out of typical ego-identification[9] and victim mentality, and into soul identification and an empowered spiritual/metaphysical worldview, it is important to take the next step forward and give compassion for the actual victimization that did occur in this physical reality at the level of ego. Just as in the discussion about things going wrong and not being fooled by the silver lining, we don't have to self delude anymore. We don't have to hide this other layer of reality behind a positive attitude or spiritual truths. We are strong enough now to feel the anger, feel the pain, feel the confusion and the fear, feel all of it, and to mourn what was taken from us. We don't have to use spiritual and metaphysical concepts to avoid this pain or transcend the physical reality we used to be stuck in. These truths have their place and serve a powerful purpose, but just because they are empowering and help us feel better does not mean they are the whole thing. It is just one layer of reality, not all of it.

As we are able to embrace the full and more complex reality of the victim paradox, we can gain the benefits of soul identification while simultaneously avoiding some of the problems that arise if we only embrace the spiritual/metaphysical view and live in a victimless world.

In a world without victims we run the risk of "blaming the victim". If that victim is us, we can blame our self for things that we shouldn't and we can let perpetrators off the hook too easily, not holding them accountable for their actions. We take on their "stuff" and blame our self for it, sometimes not even getting out of really destructive relationships. Or, in a really perverse misapplication of these spiritual truths, we might self-delude our self into thinking some of our own pathological behaviors are OK. We may be taking advantage of someone in some way and the whole time be thinking that they are creating their own reality. They are empowered people living their truth and we are living our truth. We might say to them in our mind or in real life "Don't blame me for your problems. You're not a victim." That's a lie. Plain and simple.

Besides blaming the victim, we also run the risk of not giving a victim enough compassion or proper care, items which are very important in their healing process. And again, this is true whether the victim is us or someone else.

Also, if we live in a victimless world we might be in denial and not be able to see the perpetrator for who and what they are as well. It can be scary or painful to look deeply into the darkness of a pedophile, a rapist, a sociopath, a thief, or a murderer. It can be especially difficult or confusing when this person seems normal and good on the outside. When this person is a friendly neighbor or someone who works with you. Or worst case, lives with you. Seeing their true level of pathology[10] and their true darkness may be too intense for you to deal with, so you don't see it. Just like you don't see victims, you don't see the perpetrator, or you only catch a glimpse of the perpetrator, trying to look away as if your eyes would get burned staring into the sun. When you look deeply you may see a dark entity or a demon inside of them, and you certainly don't want to see THAT!

That layer of reality may be too much for you right now. And, if that's true, that's OK. I only want to see what I'm ready to see in my life, and I only want you to see what you're ready to see in your life. There is no pride in any of this. We are where we are in our development and are ready to see what we are ready to see. In a victimless world though, we risk not seeing a lot of things that are real and that do impact us, our reality and other peoples' realities. And, even though some of these things might be painful or difficult or challenge what we thought we knew about life and the universe, that's OK. Actually, that's better than OK. That's growth.

chapter 4.

You can be highly evolved spiritually and still have major blind spots and pathologies. You're still human after all. Try not to forget this.

In fact, the further you are on your path, the more likely it is that you will find significant, often painful blind spots and become aware of deeper, stronger but possibly more subtle pathologies. Unless, of course you have already achieved full and abiding enlightenment. Otherwise, all the work you have done until now has been preparing you and making you strong enough to deal with the next and bigger challenge, the one you weren't ready to deal with before. As we've already discussed, your mind protects you from things you aren't ready for yet, so it reasons that the more you develop, the more advanced you become in your training, the more you are able to deal with.

Don't be discouraged by this dynamic. This doesn't mean that life has to be a constant, never ending series of bigger challenges that stretch us to our limits and push us to go that much deeper into our core. We don't have to go from climbing one steep mountain to the next. There are beautiful valleys at high elevations we can spend time in, and we might decide to stay for a while on a peaceful plateau with fantastic views, consolidating and enjoying the benefits of our past efforts. It is only required that a few of us deal with a constant deluge of major challenges, and if you're one of these people, then this is good news too. It means you have the capacity to handle it, and you are having the opportunity to clear out more and bigger chunks of karma and move that much deeper into the Light that much more quickly. This doesn't mean you're better than everyone else though. Please don't go there. If you thought that, you'd keep on attracting these intense growth crises just to continue to support your sense of superiority, and your sense of superiority would clearly then be a case of self-delusion.

Are you starting to get the sense of how there are traps all around us? How easily the mind can trick itself into illusions, flawed thinking and thought patterns that don't serve us? This life, this being spiritual and conscious can be tricky sometimes. It's important as we continue to develop, to be increasingly aware of our thoughts as they are happening, and to be able to go into observational mind[11] at any second throughout the day. Whether you meditate for an hour every morning on a cushion or not at all, the goal is to be able to bring an ever-growing level of awareness and consciousness into everyday, ordinary life. Sure, we can go through our days in normal awareness and then become conscious once we sit on our pillow at night or the next morning. It is better to become conscious sometimes rather than not at all. Ideally, however, we are conscious and aware all the time, or rather our heightened awareness is idling in the background all the time, forever vigilant and knowing when it needs to come in and take over our ordinary awareness based on certain situations or cues. It's not that we have to spend all of our waking hours in our observational mind and not be fully engaged in physical reality and normal, ordinary awareness. It's that our observational mind is always present even if in the background, like a watchdog looking for intruders. No intruders. No barking. But when an intruder comes in, there is barking, and we can become aware of the issue and address it at that time or as soon as we can take a break from work or caring for our child. Because we are aware of the intruder, we don't have to let them in. We don't have to identify with and act out from the wound that is trying to take us over, from the pathology, from the unhealthy thought pattern that was just about to step in and run our lives for the next five seconds or five minutes. We can hold the intruder at the gate and stop the action, and then when we have some time, we can examine the pathology, the wound, the thought pattern. We can transform it all at once by our self or over time with the help of teachers or friends. We can see where there is a hole in our fence and work to mend it, so it is no longer an avenue for other intruders to enter. This is a process, and it can take some number of years, or some number of lifetimes. Perhaps you have already done so much, it will only take you some number of days, hours, minutes or seconds.

When we are beginners, it might be overwhelming and too much to bear to see the tattered state we are in. To see all of our pathologies all at once. To see all of our flawed thinking and distorted thought patterns that are causing so much suffering in our lives and the lives of others, to all sentient beings. When we are a beginner and just getting our strength, suddenly realizing that 90% of our reality is false and a lie, might be too much. Our nervous system might not be able to handle it. We might have a total breakdown, or we might harm our self or someone else in a blind rage or in terror, or while trying to maintain our sense of security by violently forcing the external world to conform to our inaccurate view of it. We might throw our hands up in despair and not even start the journey because we see that it is too much, and we can never complete the task in this lifetime. As beginners, we may not realize the timelessness of our souls, and decide if we can't complete the task in this lifetime what is the point anyway. Let's bliss out on drugs or sex or dancing or food and just enjoy this brief life in avoidance of reality and not getting any closer to our wholeness and completion. Let's avoid seeing or dealing with these things by occupying our attention with work or watching sports on TV.

It is a good thing we don't see the whole thing at the beginning. Completion is calling us forth by showing us one step at a time. By showing us what we are ready to see and deal with. Don't feel bad or get down on yourself when, after making a huge transformation, you see another huge obstacle in front of you, or in fact, inside of you. I know it can be tiring and sometimes feel futile. But it's not. Things are getting better, and you are getting closer to something. And in the meanwhile, you are experiencing deeper aspects of your Self and Reality all the time. It is not all about the destination or the journey. They are both essential and inextricably linked. And the journey towards completion is the best and only one. And no matter how close you are, you may realize you have some pretty massive blind spots and deep pathologies. It's OK. It's all OK after all. Right? Take a deep breath and smile. Life is good.

chapter 5.

KARMA ISN'T JUST about what we do; it is also created by what happens to us.

Often times when something bad happens in someone's life, we might think that person has bad karma. They must have done something bad earlier in life or in a previous life, and now they are reaping the negative consequences. While this may be true, there is another possibility that is equally probable. It could be that something bad <u>happened to</u> that person earlier in life or in a past life, and now they are reaping the negative consequences.

Huh? I don't understand.

While the first and more common approach to how we think about karma appeals to our sense of justice, meets our need to believe that injustices are punished somewhere somehow even if not in a way we can see, and meets our need to think that life is fair, it is only half the story.

But, it wouldn't make sense for life to treat someone badly just because they were treated badly before, because something bad <u>happened to them</u> before. After all, they didn't DO anything to deserve this. How can this be karma?

The Law of Attraction and metaphysical causation come into play here. When something bad happens to us, something very bad, so bad that it wounds our soul, this wound is carried forward in our life and into future lives until it is surfaced and healed. Since the universe, primordial consciousness, wants us to be healed and whole and for our souls to be pure balls of light, it has set things up so that our wounds keep on attracting people and situations that reveal our wounds to us, so we can heal them and move on. So, when we DO something bad or very bad, we are acting out from one of our wounds and creating bad karma for our self, which simply means we are strengthening that wound by being its slave and that wound then will attract bad things to us, will continue to provide us with increasingly negative feedback about our internal state until we can see the wound and clear it. On the other hand, even if we don't DO anything bad but when something very bad is done to us, that creates bad karma as well. That wounding of our soul carries forward and attracts bad things to us, continuing to provide us with increasingly negative feedback about our internal state until we can see the wound and clear it[12].

Often times when working with past lives we will find mirror images in multiple lives. A pattern will form. Perhaps in one past life you were a victim of sexual abuse and in the life before that you were the perpetrator. These are different aspects of the same wound, creating a pattern, and each branch of that tree, each side of that coin is simply a different face of the same root cause. Karma is about cause and effect after all, but sometimes we get confused about the actual cause. The bad behavior isn't the cause, it is actually first an effect from something deeper, the wound, and then the behavior itself becomes a cause in the never ending cycle[13].

The cycle in fact does have an end though. We can clear our bad karma[14] and we can stop creating new bad karma for our self. And, whereas most people try to create good karma by DO-ing good things and avoiding DO-ing bad things, it is equally important to not let bad things happen to you anymore.

If someone is trying to steal from you in a way that would deeply hurt you and potentially wound your soul, it is very important to fight and defend yourself and not allow this to happen to you. If someone is trying to physically violate or harm you or wrong you in any way that could have significant implications for your life and possibly damage your soul, it is extremely important that you do everything in your power—within certain boundaries—to defend yourself and not allow this to happen to you. Defending yourself in a way that does not harm others will not create bad karma for you and can prevent you from getting the additional bad karma that would have resulted had the transgression occurred.

Even if you have to cause the perpetrator pain in defending yourself, this is OK too, as long as you are not actually hurting them or damaging their soul. It can be painful when we see our mistakes and pathologies. This doesn't hurt us, it actually helps us. Causing another being pain does not necessarily hurt them. Done properly, when you defend yourself you are actually helping everyone involved, even if they don't realize it. When you save yourself from being wounded again you are giving the otherwise perpetrator an opportunity to see and clear their karma and helping them break their patterns, as well. They probably won't thank you for this tough medicine, and you don't need their thanks anyway.

What I am writing about here can be pretty slippery and can be dangerous if you misapply what I am saying. You are not 007, and this is not a license to kill—figuratively or literally. When you are in a fight or flight situation and you can't run, or you otherwise realize it serves your highest good and the highest good of all beings to stand and fight—not allowing yourself to be wounded or intimidated again—it can be a very difficult situation. Your judgment may be impaired because you are angry or in a state of rage. What I am saying here does not give you permission just to act out from your anger and harm the other individual under the cover of so-called self-defense. What I am telling you, is that in order to break some of your deepest karmic patterns you must attain a level of mastery that you may not have attained yet.

Sometimes you must stand and fight, but fight in a very specific way, not in the way we normally think about fighting or see fighting portrayed in the movies or on TV. You must be able to breathe through the fight and flight response, you must be able to work that anger, rage or terror out on your own or with a teacher or healer, and then from a place of neutrality and following Divine guidance and intuition, it will serve you and everyone involved for you to defend yourself without harming others. That anger, rage or terror in the fight or flight response may be part of your woundedness, and if so, taking action from that place only makes these wounds and their accompanying karma stronger. It binds you more deeply. But, to the extent you are able to get to neutrality and defend yourself from your clear center, this is a wonderfully positive and powerful thing to do. If you are successful in this task, you can transform some deep karma once and for all and move on to bigger and better challenges. You will break that specific pattern once and for all and you will no longer be victim or perpetrator in that specific drama.

We must not allow our self to be perpetrator or victim. Each side of the drama is equally important to avoid.

In the process of taking action to defend our self or avoid bad things in the physical world, we very well may need to turn some attention inward, find the root cause of this karmic pattern, the root of the wound, and transform it with our loving, compassionate heart. And while there may be some internal work to do, please don't fall into the trap of thinking all you need to do is process, thinking you don't have to stand up for yourself and fight. Sometimes, many times in fact, it is absolutely essential to take action in the physical realm in order to get the internal shift. Sometimes healing and change comes from the outside in, not the other way around. What happens here on planet earth right now, in this life, in this body does in fact touch our souls.

chapter 6.

EGO IS NOT the enemy. When you think it is, that is your ego talking anyway.

My impression is that the ego is the most often referenced and most often misunderstood construct in all of the spirituality literature that I have seen. Sure, it is good to be able to transcend the ego, break the illusion of separation, and experience oneness with God and the universe. Yes, it is definitely a trap to act out from our wounded egos, from our pathologies that cover up our beautiful souls and spirit. It is absolutely hugely limiting if we can only experience reality from the standpoint of the ego, from the perspective of the little me, in this little body with only a tiny little window out into the vastness of the universe. AND, our egos absolutely exist for a reason and are not the enemy. What's the expression? Hate the crime not the criminal. The Truth is that a vast majority of people on this planet have egos that are less than 100% healthy, so when we see unhealthy egos acting out all the time and creating all sorts of problems, we begin to make the perceptual error of seeing ego as the problem.

Ego is not the problem. Wounded ego acting out is the problem.

This type of thinking is very egoic anyway. What is the structure that sees things as problems, resists and fights things? The ego, of course. It is sadly ironic that so many people on a spiritual path are engaged in a battle in which they are trying to overcome their egos, trying to defeat their egos, trying to dissolve out or otherwise negate the existence of their egos. The part of them engaged in these battles is their ego. All of these well-meaning people on an earnest spiritual path are stuck because their ego is in conflict with itself. This inner egoic conflict takes a lot of energy and doesn't get anyone anywhere at all. It is like a dog burning off lots of energy and calories by chasing its tail. I would recommend to any of you that find yourself in this situation, to take a step back and reconsider the situation, to stop chasing your tail.

I believe a useful analogy when thinking of the ego is one of our physical body being like a cell, and our ego is like a cell membrane. The cell membrane performs some incredibly important functions, and the cell cannot live without it. Without the cell membrane to provide a boundary between the inside of the cell and the rest of the world, that cell would not be alive. Its ingredients could be there floating around as an unstructured mass of cytoplasm, proteins and all the other items that make up a cell, but it would have no life. Sure, the cytoplasm might enjoy the ecstasy of being one with the surrounding environment, but living in the state of pure consciousness does not require a human body or human birth. We are born in this human body for a reason, and this human body needs an ego to function in this physical reality.

Our ego, like a cell membrane can have pathologies though. Perhaps the cell membrane is not good at allowing nutrient into the cell. Perhaps it is fooled by pathogens that it mistakes for nutrient and it lets inside, only to find the pathogen destroying and killing the cell. Perhaps the cell membrane is too rigid, so the cell has trouble squeezing through tight quarters and sliding by other friendly cells that are able to adapt their shapes to accommodate movement. Perhaps the cell membrane has some debris stuck to it that is blocking important receptors. Perhaps it has a problem ejecting waste from inside of the cell. In each of these instances, we might look at the cell membrane and think it is causing all sorts of problems. *Cell membranes must be bad. I want to get rid of mine.* The reality is the cell membrane is totally, absolutely 100% essential for sustaining life. The reality is that it is responsible for so many functions, and it is exposed to so many difficult environmental factors all the time—from both the inside and the outside—that a lot can go wrong. A totally,100% healthy, perfectly functioning cell membrane is a rare and beautiful thing.

I believe this cell membrane analogy is a useful one, which can help teach us a lot about our egos, but this analogy does break down at some point. We are not cells. And, as such, even though we need our egos, like a cell needs a cell membrane—and, even though our egos perform so many functions and are subjected to difficult environmental factors all the time, just as cell membranes are—we are, in fact, able to learn how to transcend our egos. We can find safe environments where it's OK to drop the ego and reunite our solitary consciousness with the One consciousness. We are able to have spiritual experiences that transcend ordinary, first person identity consciousness. We are able to shift out of first person and move into observational mind or soul identification, move into God consciousness and take various journeys with our conscious awareness.

And while there are these important differences, there are more similarities as well. Like cells, we are able to repair our cell membranes, we are able to heal our wounded egos. Instead of hating our egos, or trying to conquer our egos, we can choose to love our egos and heal them. I recently read <u>Journey of Souls: Case Studies of Life between Lives</u> in which the author Michael Newton indicated that our souls have egos even when we are not in our physical bodies, when we are between lives. This assertion actually makes sense to me, because when I contemplate healing the ego, what I actually see is necessary is healing the soul. They are one and the same, or rather, different aspects of a functioning whole. If to heal the ego we need to heal any wound that causes us to behave in a way that does not serve us with regards to how we relate to other people or the outside world, or heal any wound that has to do with letting go of energetic waste and allowing nutrient in, and all the analogous functions of a cell membrane—if this is what is required to heal the ego, then a lot of what we are talking about is healing our emotional, physical, mental, energetic and soul bodies. We are talking about healing all of our self, entirely and completely. And, when we are fully healed and whole, our ego will be too, and we will be glad we have one. A healthy ego can do a lot of worthwhile things, including protecting us and defending us and not allowing us to be victimized again, keeping us from continuing to reinforce and strengthen the bad karma involved.

chapter 7.

SEPARATION IS REAL and necessary. You are not God or The Source.

    While it is great to transcend the ego some times and commune with The Source, and while it is great to stay connected and keep an open channel to God and Source all the time, even when your awareness is turned outward into physical reality. While these are great things, please remember, just because you can achieve God consciousness, doesn't mean you are God. Just because you can Co-Create your reality, doesn't mean you are The Creator.
    As long as you have a physical body, separation is real, not an illusion, and you are simply you—even though you are part of and connected to something larger, and even though you can experience these transcendent realities and your consciousness can visit other times and places. Separation is necessary in order for us to live in these physical bodies and for the physical world as we know it to exist. The manifest world is one of differentiation and separation, whereas the unmanifest is the realm of undifferentiated

reality and union. As you become more skilled in the art of manifestation you will gain greater mastery of traveling through the gateway between manifest and unmanifest, aligning with and collaborating with The Source, and influencing how things manifest into this physical reality, into your life. When you get even further along your path, you will increasingly occupy manifest and unmanifest realities simultaneously. You will no longer need to actively travel between these worlds in order to manifest anything; you will just experience Source manifesting through you in each and every moment. You will simultaneously watch and live the process of the seeds you planted with conscious intention—in this life and in many lifetimes before—blossoming on their own; you will simply enjoy riding the wave and cooperating with the process of life and the unfolding of your perfect path towards the bliss of enlightenment—not struggling against it, not grasping onto sex, money, love, control or your wounds anymore.

If the books and teachers telling you that "separation isn't real it's just an illusion" are helping you break out of the solidness of the physical world for the first time and connect with and enter into Source, experiencing that layer of reality, and expanding your consciousness in that way, then this is a really good thing and an important step in your growth process. If these books and teachers are helping you see and feel how you are connected to other human beings, the planet, our natural environment and how all things and all sentient beings are connected, helping you see the spiritual truth that "all is one", helping you grasp that when you harm someone else you harm yourself, when you harm the web of life, the natural environment, you harm yourself—

Reinventing Truth

if they are helping you see these truths, then this is also a really good thing. Once you have had these realizations though, have stepped into union, have lived into the other side of the paradox—the part of reality you had been missing up until then—it's important to understand that those teachings were just a tool to help you take the next step. Nothing more, and not an absolute statement about the Full Nature of Reality.

Sometimes when people take that step into Source, into union, they fall into the trap of losing their footing in physical reality, the manifest, differentiated reality, the "real world". They go from being lost in one side of the paradox to being lost in the other side; they fall into the trap of replacing one partial truth with a different partial truth, instead of moving into Full Truth. They are confusing this new layer of undifferentiated reality with All of Reality, as if that old physical reality no longer exists, as if other people and their free will and boundaries no longer exist. And, while it might feel liberating and joyful to embrace this other part of existence for some while, experiencing being a wave instead of being stuck in the particulate reality of the physical world, being free of the pain of separation—be careful that this not become an addiction[15] for you, a way of escape and avoidance, a form of anesthesia. While it might feel good, please don't grasp onto these positive feelings and blissful experiences; please don't struggle when the natural flow of life is drawing you back into separation, pulling you forward on your path towards completion.

Eventually, whether by choice or not by choice, you will return to and have to deal with this physical reality that includes separation. And, if it is against your will, it will almost certainly not be a pleasant landing. I do not wish to motivate you by fear, since love is where I want you to make your choices from, but it is important that you understand the risks of certain behaviors. It is important you understand that using new spiritual truths and aspects of reality in order to hide from other aspects of reality and avoid dealing with difficult things does not lead to positive outcomes. It can be tough to see and think clearly sometimes, especially when we are all blissed out and in the ecstasy of union, when we are one with God, the universe and all things. It is easy to get lost in this. It is easy to escape into this alternate reality and identify with these experiences, for our ego to identify with God and The Creator, to take on a feeling of invulnerability, to feel all-powerful. Even though it is easy, especially when we are beginners, please don't get drunk on this. Drunkenness does eventually lead to a hangover, and let's hope at least that it does not lead to a fatal car accident. These journeys of consciousness are powerful, yet potentially dangerous, so please be careful. Please continuously develop your core and the depth of your grounding; and try not lose yourself entirely in these new experiences and realizations—at least not for too long, for a period longer than it serves you.

chapter 8.

YOU ARE NOT perfect just the way you are; your job is to become the perfect version of you—the real YOU—and dissolve away all the rest. The Truth is that YOU are perfect, but YOU might not be who you think you are. Who you identify with, the identity of your ego, very likely includes your pathologies, your addictions, your imperfect understanding of Truth and Reality, and thought patterns which don't serve you... among other things.

Michelango said something along the following lines about his sculptures. He said that he does not create them but rather when he starts on a new work, he can feel the already complete sculpture inside the monolith of stone, and his job is to free the sculpture from its stone prison. YOU, the capital Y-O-U perfect version of you, the future you, is the completed, beautiful, one of a kind sculpture trapped in a stone prison. The stone around YOU is your pathologies, addictions and all the rest. You—who your ego thinks you are—are the entire monolith of stone, so your ego identifies with things that are not YOU and allows these things to run your life from time to time, or worst case almost all the time. YOU took human birth in this monolith of stone and in this particular life in order to work on chipping more pieces away, to get one more step or many steps closer to revealing the perfect sculpture inside, to experience your perfection in the physical realm. So, while little y-o-u may not be perfect, there is a perfect YOU inside, and your job here in this life is to uncover it, to liberate it.

When you have developed perfect discernment, overcome all of your pathologies and addictions, cleared all of your karma, healed all of your wounds, seen through all illusion, dropped all the thought patterns that don't serve you, and brought all of your levels into perfect health and alignment (including your ego), then at that moment the little y-o-u will converge with the capital Y-O-U, there will be no stone left to chip away and you will be a fully enlightened, fully realized being in human form. That is your work here.

Yes, there is a perfect version of you inside of you, waiting to be released, and it is helping guide you on the path towards its and your liberation. Yes, where you are in that process of unfolding is completely perfect from one specific vantage point. Yes, accepting where you are in this moment instead of denying or struggling against it, can free up a lot of energy that you can redirect towards actual progress. It is better that you do not beat yourself up for your mistakes, for your addictions and your pathologies. Shame does not help you progress and move forward. Self-hatred does not help you progress and move forward.

Non-acceptance, shame and self-hatred can be huge stumbling blocks, which can in some cases contribute to a downward spiral taking you in the opposite direction of

Reinventing Truth

where you want to be going. Moving into the transcendent awareness where you can see the perfection of yourself and all things, can be a wonderful tool in helping you move into acceptance and drop the shame and self-hatred. However, trying to set up camp or even permanent residence in that place and from that vantage point rationalizing that acting out from your addictions and pathologies is perfect—this itself is one of the most dangerous traps, one of the worst forms of self-delusion, one of the most damaging addictions and pathologies in that it enables and amplifies all of the others—creating an incredible amount of bad karma for everyone involved.

One of the most important benefits of meditation is that over time you can and will develop greater discernment, gain greater facility in being able to consciously choose and shift that which you identify with, and continuously grow your capacity to breathe through and release bigger and bigger blocks, bigger and bigger chunks of stone covering up the perfect version of you. When going into observation mind for example, you can learn to stop identifying altogether with the normal, everyday you who you normally think you are. You can watch yourself from outside of yourself sitting on that cushion breathing, and when that body feels pain after sitting motionless in a meditative position for some period of time, you can gain skill in not identifying with the pain, not identifying with that body, and instead seeing the pain as a sensation that eventually passes.

What I am talking about here is really a form of, or at least very similar in some ways to dissociation, something that often happens to people who suffer deeply traumatic events, such as physical or sexual abuse as a child. While dissociation is a wonderfully useful, unconsciously triggered coping mechanism to protect us from fully experiencing something we are not yet able to deal with, non-identification is a conscious choice with a conscious purpose on our path of progress.

As you gain greater facility in not identifying with thoughts, emotions, and physical sensations in the body, a really wonderful thing happens. You gain more choice and more freedom in your normal, ordinary life to be who you want to be, think what you want to think, say what you want to say, and behave how you want to behave. When someone pulls out in front of you in traffic, you feel that anger start to take control of your body… but wait, you can choose not to identify with this feeling and breathe and release it. When your spouse says something that hurts your feelings, you can feel the hurt coming in and your old habit of reacting with an insult about to take over… but wait, you don't have to allow that thought and behavior pattern, those feelings and the habitual reaction, to take over your body, take over your thoughts, speech and actions.

The more skill you gain in this area, the deeper you can go, the more choice you have, and the more YOU can be at cause in your life. The more conscious you become through your spiritual practice, the more you can discern between thoughts that serve you, and old thought patterns that might have served you twenty years ago but really have no place anymore[16]. The more you can see that some thought patterns are not even yours and have, in fact, been put in your head by your parents, the media, your friends, or some other specific person or thing. The more you can discern between different qualities of thoughts, between the noise of obsessive thinking, the low quality of mundane thoughts, and the purity of inspired thought, of clear vision, of wisdom. And, as you cut out more and more of the noise, you make more and more space for the purity of wisdom to shine through. You see that these are your REAL thoughts coming from the real YOU, and that much of the chatter is little pieces of the stone prison.

And, you may also begin to see some particularly pathological, flawed thought patterns that were part of how you always saw the world, part of what you always knew to be true, thoughts you were so sure of you never even stopped to question or examine them… you might suddenly see that these thoughts come from woundedness or ignorance or hate, and you can choose not to identify with them anymore either. You can choose to no longer give them power over you. And, once they lose their power over you, and once you stop identifying with them and handing yourself over to them, they grow weaker and weaker and eventually dissipate in their entirety. Congratulations. You just dissolved a big chunk of rock covering up the perfect YOU stuck inside.

chapter 9.

DON'T ALWAYS TRUST yourself above all others.

When you are a beginner, when you do not yet have good discernment, sometimes you don't actually know what's best for you. Sometimes, you don't realize that you are acting out pathology and woundedness. Sometimes you don't realize an addiction has taken you over and is running you.

Gurus are not a popular thing in our Western, individualistic culture. The idea that someone other than our self actually knows what is best for us more than we do our self, is something that many people in the Western World are not comfortable with. The fact is, sometimes someone else does know what is best for us, more than we know our self. The role of the guru in the Eastern traditions is to illuminate the path and help us take the right steps, even in spite of our self. Full surrender to the guru, total trust, handing oneself over entirely is absolutely essential for the process to work. It is in our moments of greatest resistance when the guru can be of the greatest value. If it is a fully enlightened guru, it will very likely be exactly at our moments of greatest resistance to what they are telling us to do that we are in fact touching and with their help resisting our deepest pathologies, breaking free of our deepest patterns and addictions, taking the most powerful steps forward towards full liberation from suffering, towards enlightenment.

Even though gurus may do all these good things, as a general rule, I do not recommend that you go find yourself a guru. Typically, a student might get to know a teacher for some number of years before even considering entering into a guru type relationship. This is not something to take casually, and there are very few—if any—people alive today that would be worthy of this level of trust. Furthermore, there are a number of potential issues and built-in traps with the archetypal guru/disciple relationship, and in any case, you very likely don't need a singular guru in physical form to help you overcome pathologies and achieve enlightenment. God or The Source or The Perfect Y-O-U inside can be your guru and can speak to you and show you things through many avenues—through spiritual teachers and human gurus for sure, and also through friends and family members, therapists, colleagues, your attorney, books you read, personal or professional mentors, people on the street, songs on the radio, a barking dog, or in any number of different ways.

I only mention the archetypal guru relationship because it illustrates how it can in fact be beneficial to trust someone more than yourself. It's as if you need to trust yourself enough to know when to hand yourself over to someone else's care. There may be moments when it is in your best interest to temporarily surrender your will to the will of another human being. Perhaps there is a moment when you surrender to your spouse and trust that Divine Wisdom is coming through them and leading you on your joint Divine Path. Perhaps a friend organizes an intervention, confronting you with the loving intention of freeing you from your sex and love addiction, and perhaps even though you can't see it because it is a big blind spot, perhaps you trust them and the words of your other friends present more than yourself, and you take the first steps in the process of working through this hidden addiction. Sometimes, many times in fact, we have to start the recovery process to even see the addiction. And, in that moment of blindness, we have to trust someone more than we trust our self, more than we trust our senses, to take those first steps.

Just as it is a trap to trust yourself above all others always, the converse also comes with its dangers. You must be very selective and very discerning when you decide to trust someone else in this way. Handing yourself over to the wrong person in the wrong situation can be very dangerous and lead to very negative consequences.

You might see a recurring theme here as it relates to discernment. So many of these traps really boil down to discernment. It's as if there is one spiritual teaching telling you it is always best to turn right at the corner, and here I am telling you about a number of times when turning right can get you into trouble, so you need to turn left sometimes. But, there are times when turning left can get you into trouble too. So, what do you do? What is the rule?

The Truth is, there is no rule.

My best advice to anyone on a spiritual path is to surrender to Divine Will and in that surrender process ask for the discernment and courage to follow what the voice tells you. And, if you are not comfortable with the concept of Divine Will, then surrender to your Highest Self, to your Highest Good, to the most perfect, totally healed and whole, and conscious version of yourself, to your Divine Mind or the Buddha Mind, or to whatever other label you would ascribe to what I am referring to[17]. All of these that I mention here are in fact the same thing. And, once you surrender and ask for discernment and courage, you must develop these things. Discernment can be developed through meditation and in real life, learning to go deeper into and trust Spirit and your intuition when making decisions, small and big.

The Truth is there are so many pitfalls along this path of liberation and enlightenment, that not I nor anyone else can identify all of these traps for you in advance and tell you how to handle the situation. There are no simple rules, only in this case key guiding principles[18]. If you are surrendered to Divine Will and have increasingly perfect discernment, you have an amazing journey ahead and are certain to reach your goals… eventually. This does not mean you will never get into trouble, but it does mean that you are on your path, and while on your path, amazing things will happen and the support you need will always, always arrive.

chapter 10.

W̲H̲E̲N̲ ̲Y̲O̲U̲ ̲T̲H̲I̲N̲K̲ you've overcome dualistic thinking, you probably haven't.

When you get to the place where there is no good and evil, no self and other, and when you are able see these things as judgments and illusions—you will very like reject the old reality you used to live in where these things actually existed. In your new reality, none of these things are real, there are no opposites, nothing is separate, and all things come and return to the same source and are part of one unified whole. Hurray! You have overcome dualistic thinking.

However, to the extent you are now firmly rooted in this non-dualistic experience of reality, you have actually engaged in a different type of dualistic thinking. Just as you used to believe something is either good or evil, self or other, it can't be neither or both at the same time; now, in your apparently "enlightened" non-dual state of observation, you are, in fact, on one side of a new and more subtle "either/or" proposition—reality is either dualistic or non-dualistic, it can't be neither or both at the same time.

Now that I am pointing this out to you, you may immediately recognize that how you think about duality sounds a lot like how you used to think about any number of false dualities you have seen through in order to come this far on the path. The good news then, is that since you've already learned how to transcend these types of dualistic thought patterns, and since you are gaining greater facility in embracing paradox, it should be fairly easy for you now to move forward into a deeper form of non-dualism, one which actually embraces dualistic reality as part of the complete and unified whole. And, from that level of realization a lot of good things can happen.

First, you won't hide behind the non-dual lens and use it as anesthesia to avoid the pain and suffering of the dualistic layer of reality. You can visit Oneness without getting stuck there or having to stay there for the wrong reasons. In your broader experience of reality, you can avoid falling into the trap of letting evil deeds and wrongdoing continue to go on around you, all the while consoling yourself by escaping into some fantasy world where good and evil do not exist, doing nothing to change what is happening in "the real world" around you.

Furthermore, when you occupy a reality that has space for dualistic and non-dualistic realities co-existing as part of a richer, more complete whole, you can move freely between these worlds as necessary and as it serves your highest good and the highest good of all beings. Over time you can gain increasing skill in living in both of these seemingly contradictory layers of reality at the same time. And, to the extent that moving into Oneness gives you strength, is part of your healing process and helps you clear out blocks and negative karma—to the extent this is true, then when you operate in the more mundane reality of good and evil and self and other, you will be able to be a more powerful and effective agent in accomplishing good deeds.

You can engage in this level of reality without getting so caught up in the drama of it. For example, you will be able to engage wrongdoers with compassion. Whether it is the real estate developer destroying the local environment, the political leader utilizing misinformation and scare tactics to support a morally repugnant agenda, a nation engaged in human rights abuses, or whoever else the wrongdoer might be—you can recognize yourself in them, recognize your shared origins and destiny. You can battle their pathologies and delusion, their ignorance—not them—compassionately battle on behalf of them actually, making every effort to bring their light to the surface, even while taking action to protect yourself and others from their unconscious behaviors, from their darkness. You can engage them either directly in physical reality and/or indirectly through the world of spirit, and whichever avenue you take, you are able to move away from old dualistic mindsets that have led to so much physical and spiritual violence and destruction, so much unnecessary physical and emotional suffering, for so many thousands of years. You can move away from paradigms of destroying the other and conquering the enemy. You are no longer in the dualistic illusion that these types of behavior somehow solve problems, somehow serve you—the illusion that the enemy is actually out there, separate from you and not part of you. You recognize that much of the battle is actually inside, that you must heal your own wounding so you are not acting out your own wounds, your own karma, and making the situation worse in spite of your best intentions. At some point you may recognize that there is actually no battle anymore, no need to struggle anymore. You can effortlessly bring about meaningful change in your outside world simply by going more deeply into the light within, by dissolving out your own darkness and wounds you are seeing reflected around you in other people who are not actually other or separate. You can draw forth their light by going more deeply into your light because you understand on one level that it is the same light. You realize that not only is there no battle and no struggle, there is actually no enemy either.

By shifting your perspective and being able to stay centered in non-dualistic reality even as you navigate ordinary reality and take actions to draw forth more good and justice in the "real world"—you can be a powerful force of change, a peaceful warrior of light, helping bring about transformations that break deep karmic patterns for you and everyone involved, transformations that pull you and all of us further forward on the path of progress. Your transcendent experiences and perception of non-duality actually empower you and make you more effective when you choose to work to effect change in everyday, ordinary reality—and this is a very good thing for you and everyone else.

chapter 11.

POWER DOES NOT corrupt. Power reveals.

There are many people who are attracted to a spiritual path to begin with because things aren't working well for them in their lives, and they are looking for answers. Part of what is not working for many of these people is that they have difficult and frustrating experiences in life that they would not have if they had more money or more worldly power. They feel powerless in their lives, and they feel this way because on one level of reality it is true. They seek a spiritual path to develop one type of power—power over themselves, their feelings, their thoughts, how they respond to their every day realities—spiritual or personal power—but at the same time many of these people, even as they grow in their spiritual power, reject worldly power. They have been led to believe, most likely by their powerless parents or other powerless and bitter people in their lives, that power corrupts. Absolute power corrupts absolutely. Their belief has been deepened and fortified by seeing consistent news reports and stories of powerful people being indicted on corruption charges and otherwise revealed as corrupt. There it is again. Power corrupts. Sure as the sun comes up in the morning.

The Truth is that power does not corrupt any one at all, not even one iota. Worldly power is merely the ability to influence outcomes, to impact external reality, to influence other people through forms of coercion, to buy things or people we want that are for sale. Power gives people choices including the choice to do corrupt, unethical things. Many, many people when tempted with these choices will do something unethical. It's not because they have power. It's because they have a wound, they have a pathology, they are not seeing reality clearly, they have flawed thinking, they are living in illusion. The cause of their behavior is these other things, and power is what reveals these things. Power is the vehicle for these pathologies to act out. Power does not corrupt. It reveals.

Many of the bitter, powerless people in the world today, consoling themselves in their powerlessness with the idea that they are somehow better than these corrupt, powerful people and thanking their lucky stars that they themselves have very little power… many of these people would find that if they had power, they would do many of the same things. They would find out that they aren't any better than these powerful people they look down on. They would find out that they have pathologies too. And, what they also might not realize is that they are caught in a coping mechanism, caught in a form of self-delusion to make themselves feel better about their current station in life. Of course, some part within these people wants to have more power, wants to have more choice in their life

Reinventing Truth

for themselves, for their children, but they hold onto this belief system—power corrupts—which is a very limiting thought pattern standing between them and the realization of their goals. It is very difficult to draw more power into our lives if we believe it will corrupt us—assuming, of course, we do not want to be corrupted.

If you believe that you are a good person with a strong moral compass and pure intentions, then I encourage you to let go of this belief system if you have it, and to free yourself to fully accept more worldly power, more wealth, more influence as it arises in your life as you fully realize your Self and your potential in this world. Become conscious of this belief if it is there and dissolve it out, so that you are not limited in this way. And, if you are nervous that power would reveal things about yourself that you might not want to see or want others to see, then I would suggest you begin working these issues out now and dissolving out these pathologies, as well. I would suggest that you prepare yourself to be a worthy vessel of worldly power. The world very much needs more of these right now, and will need more of these in the future as well.

When a system reaches a certain level of corruption, a tipping point is reached, where the few good people left get driven out and the next generation of good people do not even enter to begin with. These dynamics usher in dark periods in whichever arenas are corrupt and which are affected by corruption. So, if we are talking about the political system, this has a pretty far-reaching impact. If we are talking about Corporate America, this has a pretty far-reaching impact. If, we are talking about the medical profession and the food industry and the pharmaceuticals industry, these too have a pretty far-reaching impact.

The point of our spiritual practice is not to hide on our cushion or our yoga mat for an hour a day and make our way through our day-to-day lives avoiding as much of reality as possible, creating a safe little cocoon for our self and maybe our family, and waiting around for all the bad people in power to destroy the environment, poison us with food, kill us with healthcare and pharmaceuticals and anesthetize everyone with the media and consumerism. The point of our spiritual practice is to become our fully enlightened, fully liberated selves one step at a time, and along the way live the very best possible lives we can in the physical plane. The point is to connect with a greater source of wisdom, intelligence, compassion, love and power than we can possibly imagine and to align our self with Divine Will, with our Highest Self, and to live our lives and take action from this place with these tools.

From this place and with this support we might find our self drawn towards positions of growing power in the physical realm, and if so, and if we are worthy of this power, and if we are pure in our intentions and working out our pathologies and working through illusion—if all of this is true, then this is a very good thing for us and for everyone else. Our worldly power can reveal our Divine Nature. Our worldly power will give us the choice to heal wounds, to bring people together, to increase health, to increase consciousness, to make compassionate yet practical choices, to bring more goodness into the world, to bring more light into the world. We already have the choice to do these things every day, regardless of our degree of worldly pow-

Reinventing Truth

er, so we don't need to go out and seek such power if it is not part of our path and if it does not call to us. Believing we need to seek and accumulate worldly power before we can start doing good in the world can be a trap too. But, for those of you who are truly called, for those of you who it is part of your path, Divine Will for your life, I encourage you to embrace power responsibly, and to do your best to realize your Divine Nature and reveal your Divine Nature to yourself and to all of us.

chapter 12.

SOME "NEGATIVE" FEELINGS are not our "stuff" and don't need to be processed away.

I am very grateful that that so many people have progressed to the level of consciousness where it has now become a common trap, a common misunderstanding, to always believe that "negative" feelings are our "stuff", showing us where we have been triggered and where we have some internal work to do. The fact that so many people understand now and automatically assume in fact that this other person's words or the event that just happened isn't making them feel what they are feeling but is actually showing them feelings that are already there, showing them where they have a wound, a raw nerve, reminding them of a trauma from the past, not actually creating a new one or causing them any harm in the present… the fact that people are conscious of this possible reality and have in fact made it their default setting when dealing with difficult things—all of this is extremely encouraging and says a lot about the collective level of progress in waking up to important aspects of reality and relationship dynamics. It seems it was not that long ago that people were totally oblivious to these aspects of reality, and that the default setting was always pointing the finger outward, always trying to fix other people and things in the outside world, instead of looking within where much of the real work needs to be done. We have come a long way in a short time. In fact, we have come so far, that people are sometimes starting to make the opposite mistake. Many of us have overcompensated. Many of us have actually started thinking that when we feel something negative that it is always our stuff, it is always about us and not about the other person, the situation, or the environment. The solution is always inner work, processing feelings, addressing our inner child, our woundedness.

This type of confusion is totally understandable and actually makes sense given the growth process that people are going through. When we first start on our spiritual path, our beautiful sculpture, the perfect version of our self, is buried deep inside many layers of rock, many layers of woundedness and pathology and false thinking, many layers of our "stuff". When we first start, when we feel negative feelings, it is often, if not most of the time, someone or something pushing on our stuff, showing it to us, so we can dissolve it away, getting one step closer to realizing our true and perfect nature. But, as we progress, we might find areas where we have already dissolved out all of our stuff, where our perfection is revealed and is shining through. As we progress further and further, we might be mostly uncovered, and where there is still stuff, there might be several areas with very thin layers. At this stage, when we feel negative feelings, it might be that we are not triggered, that this person or situation is not revealing something about our self that we need to fix. It could be that we are getting accurate feedback from our nervous system and emotional body that this person is doing something harmful to us, mistreating us in some way, or it could be that this situation is not right, that something wrong is, in fact, happening around us even if we can't name it yet with our rational minds. In these circumstances, it is better not to look inside and process; it is better to realize that you are accurately discerning that something is awry and to change the situation in the outside world. End the conversation, end the relationship, address the environmental issue. Whatever it may be. It takes a certain level of discernment and a great deal of self-honesty to be clear about the difference between when it is our stuff and when it is not. Some of our pathologies really don't want to be seen, so we can make the mistake of pointing the finger outward, when we should be looking inside. This mistake is still the most common one in the world today, but more and more people are further and further along their paths and are actually starting to make the other mistake—looking inside when the problem is in fact "out there". They are failing to see that their ego is healthy now, or at least this part of their ego, and that it is functioning properly by alerting them to some problem outside, like a cell membrane protecting the cell from a pathogen that it properly has identified and blocked out.

It is also important to understand that even at the beginning, even when we are still working through a lot of stuff, it is possible that we are both being triggered and something is in fact wrong, out there. These situations are often the most confusing and where we miss the mark. We either point our fingers outward entirely and miss the opportunity to grow from looking inward, or we take it all on our self, working things out on the inside while letting bad things continue to happen in the outside world. More than possible, this more complex reality—where it is both our stuff and something wrong "out there"—this more difficult situation to discern through is in fact commonplace. It is in these situations where we are probably at the greatest risk of being manipulated by others, who might take advantage of our "enlightened" viewpoint and be all too happy for us to look only inwards and not point the finger at them and their wrongdoing, accurately identifying their pathology that they don't want to look at or dissolve out.

Until our minds are strong and clear, until we develop increasing discernment and wisdom, until we develop the emotional and spiritual strength to see reality without need for coping mechanisms, we are always subject to manipulation by others who will prey on our blind spots and our weaknesses. Until we develop in this way, we will never be able to truly be at cause in our own lives and truly be able to show up in a powerful way in the world, shining more light into the dark areas, speaking Truth to power, helping bring others more fully into the light, helping change real people and real outcomes with real implications in the physical world around us.

chapter 13.

OTHER PEOPLE EXIST. Don't be a "spiritual" narcissist.

Sometimes people on a spiritual path get lost in metaphysical reality and get confused about the nature of reality. When they hear sayings like "You are the only one that exists. You create your own reality. Everything in your life is just a projection of you onto the mirror of physical existence."—when they hear these words, which are oversimplifications of reality that help us grasp important aspects of Reality the Way It Really Is—they make the mistake of believing these ideas completely. Their injured, underdeveloped ego jumps at the chance to live in a reality where it is finally and now backed by spiritual and metaphysical truth, finally and forever now at the center of the universe, truly the only one who exists, the only one who is real, with real needs, real feelings, real free will, real boundaries, and all the rest. The unhealthy ego co-opts these spiritual teachings to invisibly indulge some of its deepest fantasies, some of the deepest fantasies of our inner two year old.

Edward Mannix

The more complex reality that is closer to Reality As It Actually Is, is that while it is true on one level that everyone else is just a character projected into your life, your movie, by the powerful projector that is your soul—while this is true, it is also true that you are just a character projected into their lives, into their movie, by the powerful projector that is their soul. From their perspective you don't really exist either; you are just a projection. What is actually going on is that we each create and sit at the center of our own reality, and we each attract people, situations and other things into our reality so that we can see our self in the mirror of the external world, experience our Self through relationship with Other. It doesn't mean that these things, these other life-forms we are projecting, attracting in, aren't real. It just means they exist in our reality to show us something about our self and about the True Nature of Reality. It also means that the way they are showing up in our reality is a reflection of our inner world, a reflection of the health or woundedness of certain aspects of our souls. And, just as we are drawing forth and helping shape them, they are doing the same thing to us. This dynamic is important to understand and has many profound implications.

When someone is in our field, they are acting out scripts from our movie, scripts in our subconscious, imprints on our soul projecting out into reality. People are not solid and don't exist in the objective, solid way we often perceive them to exist (but they still exist! Just not in the way many people think they do.). People are malleable within certain limits, limits which are often far wider than we see or understand. It's as if our scripts are software programs or viruses, and we are constantly releasing all of them into our field, and when someone comes in that has compatible hardware, the virus will take hold and start running them. If we have a wound about being abandoned by men, that script, that virus, will find a suitable character to play that role, a suitable host to run that program. The same exact person that shows up in your life, gets close to you and "abandons" you—either in fact or only in your mind—that same person could have behaved very differently, could have shown up very differently had you not had that wound, had you not been unconsciously putting that program out into your field. They could have gotten close and not abandoned you, or maybe they would have never come close enough to begin with, maybe they would be an acquaintance, just someone you play tennis with once a month—depending, of course, also on what the range of possibilities are for them in their life, based on their scripts, based on their karma, as well. Or maybe had you already worked out your abandonment issues, rewritten this program, they are someone you would have never met.

And while you are creating your reality and in some real sense creating or at least drawing forth specific aspects of these people who show up in your field, it is important that you remember that they are real, they have souls, they have a field and free will too. It is important that you do not behave as if they are just illusions, figments of your imagination. It is important you don't use these spiritual teachings to justify being inconsiderate of others' needs, or worse yet justify pathological behaviors where you violate their boundaries, violate their free will, treat them as less than fully human, fully Divine.

Furthermore, while you are putting all manner of scripts and programs out that take over and run other people, the same thing is happening to you all the time. It can be startling to realize just how much it really takes to be at cause in our lives. Not only do we have to be conscious and powerful enough to avoid acting out our own wounds, our own subconscious scripts, but also we must be conscious and powerful enough to avoid acting out the wounds and subconscious scripts of other people! And, while most often it is the programs of those closest to us that have the greatest chance of running us, that have the largest impact on our thoughts and behaviors, on our lives, many times the programs of people we barely know or don't know at all also come into play.

There are many, many layers to all of this, and what I am talking about here is not just psychological things, things that function at that level. While there are many important dynamics that operate at that level, what I am talking about is deeper than that. What I am talking about is causation that happens outside of time and space, that is not dependent on action, reaction, and a chain of events that unfolds in ordinary reality and which can be explained with psychological models of cause and effect and interlocking wounds or some such thing. What I am talking about is how we draw forth reality in real time at the most basic level, about how consciousness and we as conscious beings draw forth reality into the physical plane, and how each of us exerts influence on and is influenced by everyone else in real time. How all the billions of people on the planet and actually more broadly the trillions of life forms all are interconnected at the level of consciousness, at the level of constant real time creation of reality, the drawing forth of reality from the unmanifest to the manifest, how we are all co-creating each other and our shared reality all the time, in each moment.

When we catch even a glimpse into how we are co-creating each other all the time, how all of our interlocking light and darkness, health and wounds, all of our interlocking karma fits together like a trillion puzzle pieces that aren't solid but are constantly in flux and changing and growing, how all of these interlocking pieces are drawing forth themselves and each other, and how the whole system is set up so that all of them are constantly or eventually coming a little further into the light, constantly or eventually knowing themselves and Reality a little more deeply, constantly or eventually taking one more step towards full enlightenment, towards merging with and realizing they are an expression of Divine Consciousness, the mind of God—when we see this in our mind, and when we know and feel this reality to be true in our body for even one moment, this is a powerful thing.

The day after I began writing this chapter in this book, I not coincidentally was working with a woman we will call Judith, and in our session abandonment issues came up for her. Her mother unexpectedly died not too long ago while her husband was already dying a slow death, and we quickly were able to identify the first and strongest time she had experienced abandonment in this life time—where the wound, where the karma originally came from or was entrenched in her psyche, into her neural pathways in this lifetime at least—and we were able to pull out and work with this wounded little girl inside of her and dissolve out much of this karma, heal much of this wound, before integrating a healthier and more healed little girl back into her again at the end of the session. This woman is herself a healer and well-aware of the metaphysical reality we live in, and she asked me after the session why her mother suddenly died when her husband was in the process of dying, if I thought it was somehow her karma causing this. I told her it was her wound projecting into reality in a strong way to get her attention so she could heal it and clear it out, and I was also quick to clarify that it couldn't have happened that way had it not been her mother's and husband's karma too. I wanted to immediately preempt the possibility that her mind would go to the dark place of blaming herself and her wound for their deaths. I told her it was interlocking karma. It was part of how it was set up before they came into this life, so they could all work through their karma together. While what I told her is true on one level, I was left feeling uneasy after our conversation, like there was something more. I had provided the best response I could in real time, but her question had hit the frontier of my understanding in that moment. While I had already been thinking about this topic, I hadn't fully formulated my thinking in this area, so I continued looking more deeply at the issue. I later realized that the more complete answer is more complex and sheds more light on the fundamental nature of reality and this human existence, helps us understand more clearly how we all co-create each other and our shared realities together, and how this process of awakening, clearing karma, healing wounds, growth and progress works. What is behind it.

There is no doubt in this instance that her husband and her mother were manifesting their own karma through their respective illnesses, that their wounds were coming to the surface in the physical realm, at the end of the chain of metaphysical causation, giving them the opportunity to see their wounds in the most obvious and tangible way, in their bodies, so they could clear them out. And, there is also no doubt that this woman's wound was also projecting out into her field, and that her program of abandonment had found suitable hardware in her mother and husband to run that program, perhaps multiple times throughout her life or in past lives with these same souls. It is true that this program of hers, and perhaps others as well, were reinforcing the diseases of her loved ones, even while she was desperately trying to help them find healing and recovery through her conscious actions.

She concluded from her experience that as a healer you can't really help your loved ones because you are too close to it, too entangled in their process, and especially if at some level they don't really want to be helped. The Truth is she is only partially right in her assessment of the situation. The Truth is her loved ones were better off as a result of her conscious, positive efforts to bring greater healing and consciousness and love into their lives. But, in this case the collective strength of their wounds, of their karma, and the strength of the subconscious programs coming from her wounds and karma, were stronger, much stronger in the short term than her conscious efforts. This does not mean her efforts did not change the balance though, did not already bear fruit and will not bear more fruit in the ongoing life of the souls of her loved ones, in their future lifetimes.

Every action we take does have far reaching effects, typically much farther reaching than most of us ever realize. What is also true in this case, where she is partially right, is that it is difficult to be a powerful force of change in the lives of loved ones when they are activating and reflecting our wounds, when we our self are not yet completely healed, when we our self are living out our own karma and not able to clear it, which brings us to another part of the Truth.

The Truth is, had she somehow been able to heal this abandonment wound at that time or before these events ever occurred, things might have gone differently. At the least, her subconscious program or programs would not have been reinforcing the difficult karma being faced by her loved ones. At the most, she could have made a more powerful difference in their lives, been a more empowered actor and could have helped them heal their wounds and transform their karma entirely in this lifetime, could have maybe done this before the onset of their illnesses, or at early enough stages where they could have had complete physical recovery and they could have shared more and better memories together in this lifetime, in these physical bodies.

But wait, wasn't it also part of her loved ones' karma that no one showed up that could help them that way? Wasn't it part of their karma that they weren't ready to clear their karma yet?

This is also very likely true. Their karma was also very likely running a program on my client, was keeping her locked in her wound and karma, as well, limiting her level of awakening and healing and power, so she could not show

Reinventing Truth

up in that more powerful way in their lives, as a character in their movies. That more powerful version of her couldn't exist in their worlds because the wounds on their soul were blocking that character from being projected into their movies, showing up in their realities.

The interlocking karma, the level of entanglement runs deep.

But even so, things could have gone differently. Karma is not destiny. If that were so then we would be back to a mechanistic view of the universe, where original causes that happened before any of us were ever born lead through a mechanistic line of causation to unchangeable outcomes. There is no room for free will, no room for Grace. This is where we reach the limits of the accuracy of the movie projector analogy, where Reality is actually more complex than that.

Did this woman I was working with make the best possible choices in every moment in this life and in her past five lifetimes? When she made mistakes and realized they were mistakes did she extract the maximum amount of learning from them and modify her behavior as quickly and powerfully as possible in every instance? Could she have done any better in any moment? The answer is both yes and no. On the one hand she could not have done any better because if she had, she and you and I would not be living in this reality, things would be different. On the other hand, she could have done better and created a different reality in which we would all be living (or at least those of us who are incarnate in that parallel reality at this moment in time). This is also true, and on one level, in one reality, she actually did do better. The Truth is trillions of trillions of parallel realities co-exist right now based on every choice that could have been and actually was made differently by every single soul in those other realities since the beginning of time, the beginning of choice, and based on every choice that can be and actually will be made in the future by every single soul until the end of choice, until infinity. These realities exist separately, spiraling around each other in a fractal, spiral formation, and they also converge and weave in and out of one another at different points in peoples' individual lives and at different points in history, in our collective lives, giving us the opportunity to get off of our current path, change our current trajectory, and move into another reality, connect with a different line of causation.

The Truth is had she made any number of choices differently at different times in her life or in past lives, things might have gone differently. She might have cleared out enough of her karma to show up differently and help create a different outcome in the lives of her loved ones. Maybe. Depending on the relative strength of their karma and the power created by her choices. And in that instance we see another side of the interlocking karma. If her past choices had changed her karma at any moment in time, it also would have instantaneously changed the karma of her loved ones, instantaneously clearing some of their karma, as well, before it had the chance to play out and unfold in linear time, in physical reality. In this instance, she would have shown up differently in their reality, even in a way that did not fit, was not possible for their souls, even in a way which defied the programs they were putting out in the field, defied their "otherwise" karma, shining light into their reality in a way that was incongruent with the imprints on their "otherwise" film, showing up in a way that was not really possible based on the worldview that their outer world reflects their inner world.

In their realities, she would have been the Grace of God.

Her reality would have been stronger than their "otherwise" realities, would have overturned their "otherwise" realities, would have altered their realities. She would have been at cause in their lives, and at cause in a powerfully positive way. This is grace. This is a gift. This was not their karma but something stronger than their karma. And the way that she would have been able to do this would have also been based on Grace showing up at some point previously in the life of her soul. It could have been that she made different choices that were in fact outside of what should have been possible given her karma, but that she made them anyway and overpowered and cleared some of her karma, enabling her to show up in this powerful way—which on one level is also Grace—when we make choices that are greater than our karma, when our free will is more powerful than our karma. And, it could have also been that someone could have shown up in her world differently during her loved ones' illnesses or at a previous time in the life of her soul. A teacher or healer could have shown up in a way that was also beyond her "otherwise" karma, outside of what her soul was projecting into Reality, and this would have been Grace too—in her reality, from the individual vantage point of her individual existence, from the vantage point of her ego.

But, if we zoom out for a moment, and look at this from a broader perspective what looks like Grace at the individual level looks different at the collective level. It is still Grace but also something else.

It is also evolution.

It is Lamarkian evolution as opposed to Darwinian evolution[19]. It is not evolution guided by random mutations and the survival of the fittest. It is evolution based on intentional mutations, innovations in fact, new behaviors, new choices, that enable us to cope with, flourish within and/ or possibly change our environment. In this collective reality we live in, there are billions of humans bumping up against difficult aspects of their reality, of themselves, all the time. There are billions of humans that are trying to figure it out, trying to get it right, striving to fully realize them Selves and their Divine nature, experience the bliss of completion, of total healing, of enlightenment. There are billions of humans constantly adapting to their difficult environment, constantly reconfiguring themselves, thinking new thoughts, trying new actions, experimenting through trial and error. Just like single cell organisms intentionally mutating their DNA to try to find a new combination that helps them adapt to their environment, survive or even flourish in their environment—sometimes, some of these humans get it right. They find something that works. Eureka! They discover a useful innovation that helps them on their path, that makes them "more fit", that helps them clear wounds, clear karma instead of just living through it and repeating it, helps them become more powerful in a positive way. And, when this happens in someone's life, when they are the winners of the Lamarkian evolutionary lottery, it is grace. Or perhaps it is karma? Perhaps they were successful innovators in past lives, perhaps they cleared the wounds that blocked this type of spiritual, emotional, metaphysical innovation, and now they are reaping the benefits. But how did they do that to begin with? Where and when did they get on the upward spiral leading to their good fortune in this lifetime? Back then it would have also been Grace.

And when Grace shows up in one person's life it is actually showing up in everyone's life. When someone through the grace of their own inspired free will breaks through their own karma, overpowers their own karma, clears their own wounds leading them to a place where they can be at cause in their own life, not running their negative programs or anyone else's, leading them to a place where they are a powerful being of light which can show up in other peoples' fields in a way that is beyond the "otherwise" karma of those other people, when this happens, this is grace for everyone. It is the beginning of, or depending on how you look at it, somewhere in the middle of, a long chain of events, a chain of events which eventually leads to the enlightenment, to the full liberation of all beings.

When one person becomes enlightened, we all do.

Different than the process of physical evolution where there is only survival of the fittest, flourishing of the fittest, in this metaphysical reality, in the world of souls and reincarnation, in this world, even the unfit eventually become fit. Even if not in this lifetime, their souls come back again, and at some point they will be exposed to or be run by these good viruses, these good programs put out by one or more enlightened beings, programs which draw forth the very best in them, which help them heal their wounds, clear their "otherwise" karma instead of just suffering through it. Even the unfit in some lifetime will eventually either make an inspired, karma altering choice or have a powerful light bearer show up in their field—neither of which was possible based on the level of their "otherwise" woundedness, based on the "otherwise" imprints on their soul projecting into their reality. They themselves will make an inspired choice, or an extremely light and powerful character will show up in spite of their "otherwise" inner state, helping bring them up to a new level, helping them evolve and progress individually and as part of the collective evolution, the collective progress that is happening all around us all the time, and which is in fact part of the core of the fabric of life, sitting at the heart of the impulse of life, an innate part of the pure awareness, the pure consciousness that is in every moment bringing forth this physical reality that we live in.

Although it is hard to see sometimes, there is a positive bias built into the system. Evolution, progress, increasing consciousness, the journey towards full and abiding enlightenment is built in. The second law of thermodynamics as it is often understood is incorrect. Systems do not devolve from states of higher organization to lower organization. This type of entropy does not apply to living systems, which evolve from lower, simpler states of organization to higher, more complex states of organization. Living systems are the unfolding of, are the manifestation of consciousness in the physical realm. Living systems follow the pattern of the growing and the blossoming of a flower from a seed. The seed of consciousness came in, or came into this planet at least, when the first single cellular organism came to life on earth and became aware of itself and its environment. That is when the eyes of God first opened on this planet. That was the newborn baby of consciousness on this planet. And, consciousness has been evolving and taking form in more complex physical forms since with greater and more complex consciousness and perception, more complex nervous systems, greater means to realize and become fully conscious of the One Consciousness that is coming through all the time, the One Consciousness that is creating life and all that is in its own image all the time, the One Heart that is beating all of us, that is causing the unfolding of the seed of itself into the flower of all the life forms around us and this world as we know it, the life forms that will be and the world as we will know it in the future, when all beings are more deeply aware of their Divine nature, are fuller expressions of the Divine Heart, the Divine Mind, the One Consciousness that gave birth to all of us.

Intentional evolution is built in. Grace is built in.

This is a very interesting concept and understanding of life, but what do we do with this information? What do we do now to make our lives and our loved ones' lives better? To make everyone's lives better?

We draw more grace into our lives by recognizing where it is already there and feeling gratitude for it in all of its forms. We feel gratitude for the light beings that show up and work through other people in our lives—family members, friends old and new—light beings that sometimes show up as a reflection of where we are already healed, where we have already cleared our karma, and who other times show up in spite of our "otherwise" woundedness and karma, light beings who have changed our karma for us through their choices, light beings who perhaps ARE one of our friends or family members or someone else in our lives. We feel gratitude for the grace that is our free will and is our innate ability to continually reinvent our self and the way we see and experience reality. We feel gratitude that our free will can be stronger than our karma, that we have more power than our karma, our wounds. We feel gratitude for the positive bias built into the system, leading us over time through the expression of our own free will and our ability to learn from our experience, learn from our pain and suffering and from our pleasure and bliss, learn to make better choices that pull us forward more deeply into the light, bringing us one step closer to full realization and enlightenment.

We do everything in our power to become more conscious right now. To become more at cause in our lives right now. To become more healed and whole right now. To clear more of our karma and get clearer right now.

We regret the times we didn't make the best choices, didn't do our very best to be the best possible versions of our self. We feel sad about this and vow to do better in the future but we do not feel shame, hate our self or beat our self up over this.

We meditate. We learn to control our minds, instead of allowing our unconscious minds, our habitual and neurotic thought patterns to control us. We seek out qualified spiritual teachers with proper intention. We seek out healers of all sorts who can help us on different levels, on bringing light to different aspects of our being. We invest more time and energy and money in healing our self and doing the inner work we need to do because we see that this is the most important thing in both the short run and the long run. We see that it will bring us the greatest amount of joy and happiness now and in the future, it will enable us to create the life we want for our self and to more and more show up as grace in other peoples' lives, to eventually experience the joy of being the Grace of God more and more often in this lifetime or in another lifetime, as soon as we can become powerful enough, light enough.

As we work through more of our own wounds, our own patterns, our own karma, we become sensitive enough to Reality that we can be aware of the more subtle times when someone else's scripts, someone else's programs and viruses, are trying to take us over and run us. And, then we use our growing power, we use our growing clarity to see and resist that force too. We learn how to show up as we are, as pure balls of light, even when someone else's program is wanting to pull darkness out of us, even when their wounds are trying to project dark scenes into the movie of their life. We learn how to not be a bad actor, a shady character in someone else's lives but rather we become powerful enough that we are able to sometimes show up in the bad scenes to provide comfort and compassion, to help them rewrite the script, reprogram their magnet.

We do all of these things for the benefit of our self and all sentient beings. And, of course, of course, of course, it almost goes without saying at this point, we absolutely do not fall into the trap of being a "spiritual" narcissist. We understand fully and completely now without a doubt that other people do exist. They are not only projections of our soul into the mirror of our physical reality. They are also souls, and we are projections of them as well. We are co-creating each other while simultaneously both being created by the same greater or more basic consciousness underneath. As such we recognize the unity underneath the separation. We recognize our interconnected fate. We recognize that when we harm them, we harm our self. When we help them, we help our self. On one level.

We don't get carried away with all of this, lose sight of other parts of reality when embracing this spiritual reality, this metaphysical reality. We don't lose sight of the fact that sometimes we need to <u>not</u> give our food, money or belongings away to our needy friend or neighbor. We don't lose sight of the fact we need to take care of our self and sometimes Divine Will in our lives is that the only help we give to another is the support and healing force of our compassion. And, we do recognize the Divinity in all humans and in all sentient beings. We do see where they come from and where they are going. Who and what they are. Other expressions of light that deserve our respect and reverence, just as we deserve this from our self and everyone else.

Other people do exist. Don't be a "spiritual" narcissist.

chapter 14.

Awakened is not enlightened.

You may have had some awakenings or perceived awakenings reading this book, but this does not mean that you are enlightened or that I am enlightened.

You may have come across people on your journey who seemed or were in fact very awakened in some ways but who had fallen into some of the traps I have outlined in this book. Maybe they are spiritual narcissists, or maybe they believe people are perfect as they are and it is OK for you and for them to act out their addictions and pathologies.

Just because someone helps you wake up does not mean they are enlightened. Just because someone is more awake than you in certain areas and can open your consciousness to certain beneficial things does not mean they are enlightened. With almost 100% probability they are not, and it is best that you remember this. It is best that you remain skeptical and constantly evaluate and re-evaluate what they are espousing as truth and the path. It is best that you do not pick up their obscurations, that you do not become one with their mind stream entirely, picking up both the light and dark, the truth and obscurations, the clarity of their wisdom and the warping that remains in their mind stream.

Sometimes someone can have seemingly very bright, almost blinding light. You might feel yourself move to a perceived higher vibration or altered state of consciousness just being in their presence. They may demonstrate mastery over energy and consciousness that you have not come across before. They may say many things that sound very enlightened, that resonate with you on some deep level. And, even so, they might have some very dark spots. Maybe in fact, a number of big swaths of darkness that their light still hasn't burned off and that you don't notice at first because where the light is shining through it is so bright.

Just because people develop some amount of wisdom or even special abilities or powers does not mean they are pure light. Some people are born with these powers and abilities, and they do not have the proper internal or external guidance directing them to surrender themselves and all of their capacities to Divine Will, do not have the proper internal or external guidance directing them to not let their egos identify too much and take over and think they are somehow special or perfect, avoiding looking at where they still have much work to do. Some degree of power over energy and consciousness can be developed without becoming pure light, can be developed in fact with improper motivation—embracing dark motives or feeding invisible addictions. Please do not put too much stock in magic tricks or altered states of consciousness. Please try to see past these things and look at the purity of their heart, the clarity of their mind, and the ethics of their behavior and the behavior of their students.

If you come across one of these individuals with both light and shadow, you would be best be served not accepting their light or any gifts or healing from them whatsoever. You would be best served finding a purer source, not connecting with them and their mind stream in any way at all. If you find yourself lured by the light and not wanting to let it go even after you see the shadow, it could be you are in scarcity mentality about light beings. You might not know or believe that you can find powerful, very luminous teachers with proper motivation. Or maybe you are really hooked into the dark spots, they have corded into your addiction and pathology, and you are self-deluding, holding onto your own darkness and the reflection of it in your teacher under the false pretense of bathing your self in their light.

Beware of false teachers and getting caught in their shadow, and beware of picking up the small obscurations in even the brightest of teachers. As we have already discussed, you can be highly realized and still have major blind spots and pathologies. This applies to your spiritual teachers just as it applies to you. This is true whether these teachers are considered fully enlightened by every one you know, whether they are wearing robes, or whether they are levitating or walking on water.

Your job is to become more awake than your teachers—even the very bright and awake ones—to become more enlightened than your teachers—even the very enlightened ones—and to see their blind spots after they have helped you see yours. Your job is to be a master, not a slave, not a sheep, not a follower or disciple—to be the master of yourself and no one else. Your job is to do greater things than your teachers, as any worthy teacher would want their students to do, would know their students will do. Their job is to see past your dark spots, to recognize and help draw forth the Divinity in you, not the other way around… that is until you become their teacher.

chapter 15.

HALF ENLIGHTENMENT IS not full enlightenment.

Achieving absolute enlightenment and thinking it is the whole thing can be a trap. Many so called fully enlightened masters have only attained full or partial realization of absolute reality, full or partial realization of absolute enlightenment. They are only partially enlightened, and they may have very many obscurations in relative reality, a place where they might not be spending too much time or be very accustomed to at this point in their development. It may take them some number of lifetimes for this absolute enlightenment to take full expression in relative, time bound reality. Just because they can sit in their fully enlightened center, be in their fully enlightened core, sit in God Consciousness and remain there for the rest of their lives in a heightened state of consciousness, does not mean they do not have karma, they do not have wounds around the edges, or even close into the core, wounds that will show themselves the moment they exit absolute reality and engage in relative reality. It simply means that they got to the core and through the core. They got to the pure light within and beyond, beneath all the wounds and blocks, beneath their karma. They got to their non-time bound essence, their fully realized Self that exists outside of time and space and physical reality, and then beyond Self and essence in its entirety, to the place where they are just sitting in the awareness of All That Is. And just because they may have more work to do around the edges, it does not mean that Divine Will for their life might not be to sit in that space of absolute reality for their whole life or for many lifetimes showing others how to get there and burning off as much karma as they can from that place—maybe all of it. These individuals absolutely do serve an important purpose, and we should be extremely grateful they are here to hold that space and help draw forth absolute reality into relative reality for all of us, change our "otherwise" karma for us through their choices, and to illuminate important parts of the path which are relevant to both our absolute and full enlightenment. We can learn and grow very much from being in their presence and receiving their teachings and loving support.

It can take many lifetimes only to achieve absolute enlightenment, and on one level of reality, once you achieve absolute enlightenment you are actually fully enlightened. In non-time bound reality. Once you realize absolute enlightenment, it is inevitable as long as you continue to follow Divine Will and let the flower from this seed unfold through time and causation that you will eventually realize full enlightenment, that your enlightenment will take full expression in relative reality, in physical time bound reality. It might take 500 or 5,000 years to mend and transform all the potholes around your core, to burn off all your remaining karma and heal all your wounds, but as long as you continue to follow Divine Will, it will happen. Back here in time bound reality however, it actually hasn't happened yet. If you have achieved absolute enlightenment, you have created this reality in a powerful way, planted a seed in the unmanifest in a powerful way that reverberates causation backwards and forwards in time, sending out shock waves to your past, future and parallel selves and all sentient beings from all times and time lines. And, as powerful and profound as this act is, this is only planting the seed. Absolute enlightenment is the seed of full enlightenment, but it is not the whole thing. It is unmanifest enlightenment; it is not the ripened fruit.

In spite of what some teachers may tell you, at some point in your process you may need to leave the state of absolute enlightenment, the heightened consciousness of absolute reality, in order to transform the rest of your karma and achieve full enlightenment. It is important that you develop perfect discernment regarding Divine Will for your life so that you are getting your guidance directly from The Source, from your Highest Self, from God, from Divine Mind. Sometimes, Divine Mind will communicate to you through your spiritual teachers, through books, through religious scriptures—they will be the vehicle for the message. Other times, your teachers alive or dead will point you in the wrong direction, even if they are well meaning and highly realized.

The only person that can consistently know what is Divine Will for you, can consistently lead you on your Divine Path, in the right direction, is you. No one else, and I mean no one else, can show you the whole path. They may be able to point you in the right direction for several years, help you see many of your blind spots and barricades for some number of years, but they cannot ever show you the whole path. Each path of full enlightenment is fully unique, which means you cannot walk the whole path in someone else's footsteps. There may be passages where following others' footsteps is the very best way to go. We may be able to learn very much from others who have gotten very far on their unique paths. But at some point in the process, we must define and live into and allow the unfolding of our own unique process of finding our truest and purest expression, of realizing our fully Divine selves, our fully enlightened selves. And this process can take a very long time, often times longer than you will have a relationship with any one teacher.

Historically, the path to full and abiding enlightenment has taken much longer to play out in time bound reality than some of your more optimistic teachers and teachings would indicate is possible—perhaps because they are confusing absolute enlightenment with full enlightenment. While it is true that absolute enlightenment may come very quickly, the gap between absolute enlightenment and full and abiding enlightenment historically has been at least many years and often times many lifetimes. Even though the gap is shrinking now during this moment in history, and even if you made great progress already in other lifetimes—even still, it may take many years or life times for your enlightenment to take full expression in All of Reality, for you to realize full and abiding enlightenment after you have experienced absolute enlightenment.

Reinventing Truth

    I say none of this to discourage you from making every effort to attain absolute and/or full enlightenment in this life time, next week, or in this very moment even. Maybe you have achieved these before and just don't remember right now. Maybe the path is shorter than you think. And, regardless of how long it takes, taking action each day and in each moment to gain and experience full and abiding enlightenment is still the best and most worthwhile way to spend your limited time here in this physical body, to expend the finite number of breathes you will take in this physical body. Progress on the path brings many rewards and is worth any amount of effort, any amount of perceived sacrifice to follow Divine Will towards full enlightenment, even if the ultimate goal is still very far away.

    If you are already very far along your path, you may have already experienced absolute enlightenment, or you may have meaningful partial realization of absolute enlightenment. While this is exciting, please don't fall into the trap of thinking you are fully enlightened; please do not settle for absolute enlightenment and think your journey is complete (unless it actually is!). When you are in absolute reality, absolute enlightenment is all there is, but this is only one level of reality and some might argue not the most important one.

    What is the point of planting the seed if it never bears fruit that we can eat and enjoy?

chapter 16.

PRACTICING DETACHMENT IS very important, as is being attached to your physical body, your life partner and important outcomes among other things. It is no wonder so many people are confused about detachment, since resolving the detachment paradox sits at the core of straddling matter and spirit, learning to live in the world while not being of the world, gaining mastery of the middle way. Some might argue that resolving the detachment paradox represents a very high level of mastery and realization. I do not know if I would make that argument, but I do believe that this specific achievement is critical to living an aligned, happy and complete life here in the physical realm.

The reason why practicing detachment is so important, is because attachment, i.e., clinging onto things like our physical body, relationships, and material belongings for example—because this type of clinging presents perhaps the single biggest potential impediment to following Divine Will in our lives. This type of clinging potentially leads to unaligned fear and all the negative consequences that result from acting out from a place of unaligned fear.

This type of clinging ultimately leads to suffering, since all of these things we cling onto are impermanent and will change or fall away. It is no wonder that wise teachers have advised us about the dangers of attachment and that wise students do their very best to practice detachment. The problem is that just as attachment can be a trap, the indiscriminate practice of detachment, the misapplication of this useful concept, the practice of detachment to avoid dealing with difficult things in physical reality, the use of detachment as a form of spiritual escapism, the use of detachment as a rationalization to avoid intimacy and closeness with another human being or to stray from our Divine Path—these things can also be a trap.

chapter 17.

MANY PEOPLE ARE addicted to various drugs, and some of these drug addicts claim to be on a conscious spiritual path. The "conscious" drug user may set a conscious intention before using their drug of preference—most often marijuana, mushrooms or increasingly ayahuasca—so that their drug experience is guided by their intention, so that they might have certain realizations or experiences while on that drug that are consistent with what they are seeking in life, what they are looking for on their path. And, as a result, they may indeed have some very interesting, seemingly powerful realizations. Because of this, it is more difficult for them to see the Reality that they didn't need drugs to have those realizations, and they don't need drugs to have realizations in the future. Because of this, it may be more difficult for them to see that they have direct access to the Light and they don't need a plant to show them the way. It may be more difficult for them to see that they are on a false path, that they are essentially engaged in a plant based religion or cult, a type of plant worship; they are, in fact, worshiping a false idol, following a false teacher, engaged in activities that will not bring them what they are seeking in life. Furthermore, it may also be difficult for them to discern that some of the perceived realizations they are having are just that – *perceived* realizations, mirages, interesting insights that may or may not be true and in either case are simply distractions, drawing their attention and mind away from where it needs to be in order for them to truly progress on their spiritual path.

If you are one of these spiritual drug users, I hope you will read the remainder of this chapter with an open heart and an open mind. What I want for you are the same things you want for yourself – increased happiness, joy, peace, understanding, abundance, warmth, connection, community, enlightenment and all the rest. I simply have a different understanding than you do with regards to whether psychotropic drugs support or hinder spiritual awakening, a different perspective that may help you take big, non-incremental steps forward towards reaching your goals… if you are willing to be open to it, even just for the next 5 or 10 minutes as you read the rest of this chapter.

When the universe wants us to see something, when our mind wants us to see something, it will show some version of it to us through whichever doorway we give it. The forces of karma and Divine Consciousness are often times much more powerful than we are, especially when we are beginners and haven't developed our power yet. As such, there are certain things that almost regardless of what choices we make will be revealed to us in some form to some degree. In our awakenings process, there are certain pieces of information that we need at certain junctures, and they will be delivered to us in full or in part by whichever door we leave open. The Divine Intelligence, The Mind of God, *your mind*, knows exactly which piece of information you need next and will deliver as much as it can to you as clearly as possible. Your choices and the power of these choices relative to your karma and the Divine Mind will determine how distorted or clear the message is, how complete or incomplete the download will be.

When you have some version of an authentic realization during a drug experience and you attribute that realization to a substance, you are making a misattribution. That realization had to get through and is a reflection of your positive intention and where your soul is in its process of awakening and healing; and that substance was the window that worked for you given where you were and how conscious you were at that moment on your path. Had you been conscious enough to already be free of that addiction, the message, or a Truer version of it – possibly one containing only Truth without an ounce of delusion or illusion – a Truer version would have certainly come via another avenue, and one that would have served you better. When we use drugs as the window, we may not realize that other things besides what we are looking for, other things besides the perceived light and perceived realizations on which we are focused are coming through the window – dark things, things we don't want in our lives, in our minds, or in our fields. And please remember, sometimes even the perceived light and perceived realizations are just that – *perceived* mirages, illusion posing as reality, a dirty trick played on you and your life.

You may be self-deluding right now that you are not addicted to this drug or these drugs, and you sincerely use them as a vehicle towards greater health and enlightenment. Let's do a simple test right now to verify whether such a belief is true.

Imagine for a moment that instead of using that drug you could sit on a cushion and meditate for an hour and have those same realizations or Truer versions of them. Imagine for a moment that instead of using that drug you could have a one hour session with a healer and have those same realizations or Truer versions of them. Imagine for a moment that if instead of taking those drugs you could go for a walk by yourself and on that walk you would meet a fully enlightened Master, and you could have those realizations or Truer versions of them just by being in his or her presence for ten seconds. Hold your hands out palms up in front of you, and in your right hand place the drug experience as the path to realization, and in your left hand all of these alternative experiences that don't include your drug of choice, or drugs of choice. If the drug experience is still pulling on you, if there is something in your right hand that is still attractive to you, that you feel you can't get in your left hand, this pull is in fact your addiction to that drug. This pull is your hidden motive.

But, perhaps you didn't even get that far in the exercise because your mind kept telling you that you couldn't have gotten those realizations via those other methods, that you can't get realizations in the future from those other methods. You need the drug to get those realizations.

Let me tell you something very important. Those are not even your thoughts in your head. Those are thoughts those plants are putting in your head to keep you as their servant. Those plants have infiltrated your brain and are connected to certain pleasure centers and chemical processes in your brain and body. There is a hook in your brain and a cord between that part of your brain and those plants. This is the leash these plants keep you on so you continue to serve them. If you pause for a moment you may be able to see that this is literally true. It is not an analogy.

You will never, ever attain Freedom and Enlightenment as long as you are slave to a plant. It just can't happen.

As your spiritual practice grows, and through sober meditation, you can see very clearly the difference in quality between different types of thoughts. As you develop this discernment, you will see exactly what I am talking about. You will have an "aha" moment when you see that these thoughts aren't yours. They don't emanate from within you but come from the outside. You will see these thoughts are in some ways similar to the voice of your mother in your head when you make certain decisions or do certain things. You start thinking certain things, or judging things a certain way and then you realize, this isn't me thinking. This is my mother. Since those thoughts don't bring you pleasure and feed your addiction, it is easier to see they come from the outside. If not already, over time you will see the Truth in what I am saying here. You will see that these thoughts don't come from your Highest Good, the capital Y-O-U version of you, they don't come from who you really are. These thoughts and thought patterns come from the outside and become part of the stone covering YOU up, part of the stone that you are here to chip away, revealing your true and Divine nature. This addiction is part of what is covering YOU up, and it is keeping you in bondage. It is limiting your choice. Limiting your freedom, sometimes via the illusion of offering you the temporary experience of freedom. These plants are tricky little viruses that need you as a host to give their consciousness voice through you. They offer you something, certain experiences, and they give you plenty of ammunition that you can use against yourself; they support your self-delusion and give you convincing lies you can tell yourself and other people. And, even these experiences they give you, these perceived glimpses into freedom or insight, these themselves are tiny and shallow compared to what is on the other side of this addiction, what you would be experiencing if you were giving your own consciousness voice instead of serving these plants. When you are in your addiction, you are like a child looking at a sparkler, amazed by its beauty and brilliance, and meanwhile you cannot see the most brilliant firework show going on up in the sky. You are looking down at the sparkler, not up, and you have no context to understand what you are missing.

If not already, once you make some progress in this area you can start to detach from some of your past drug experiences that led to perceived realizations, and you can start to see that yes, in fact, you could have had that realization or a Truer version of it some other way. Perhaps this will be easier first with lesser realizations, and over time, if you keep looking at this, even the most intense, transcendent, breakthrough realization you have ever had or perceived you had while on drugs, you will see that you could have gotten that or something better another way, as well. You can see that these perceived realizations are silver linings, and that things went wrong, you made a mistake. You will see you could have had these realizations, or deeper, greater ones in another way. You might have a surreal moment, when you see how much you have been lying to yourself for so long, when you see that reality is so much different than you always thought and told yourself. You might feel like you are coming up out of a fog, coming into the clarity of sobriety, and you might be confused, angry, sad or just want to cry. It is important in moments like these that we feel compassion for our self, that we feel compassion for our humanness, that we feel compassion for this lost soul that is having a huge blind spot revealed to it, that is seeing for the first time that they were lost even when they didn't realize it. You are now strong enough to deal with this reality, otherwise you wouldn't be seeing it. Your loving heart is big enough now to give compassion to this past version of yourself without judgment or degradation or feeling pity.

You can send yourself compassion and heart energy as you say to yourself,

"I'm so sorry you were so lost and alone and didn't realize it."

"I'm so sorry you were a slave to this drug, that you gave your freedom and power away to this drug and didn't realize what you were doing."

"I'm so sorry that in your ignorance and delusion, acting out from your addiction, you hurt others and yourself in ways you cannot fix."

You are ready now to be free from this addiction. You are ready now to take a big step forward more fully into the light. The clear light of your own perception is the knife with which you cut away this addiction and all that doesn't serve you. Things will be different now. Not just with this, but in so many other ways. Life just got a whole lot better, including in ways that are beyond what you can possibly foresee right now. This is a truly beautiful thing. This is perfection. What you are experiencing now is healthy bliss arising from the emergence of True Freedom. Take a moment to appreciate what this feels like and to commend yourself for all the work you have done while reading this book. Take a moment in silence to dedicate all the energy you just freed up, dedicating it to achieving enlightenment for the benefit of yourself and all sentient beings.

Thank you for your work. Thank you for reading. Thank you for achieving Freedom and Enlightenment.

Part II

Commentary on Introduction

THE MOST IMPORTANT thing you could possibly do right now is to consciously and powerfully surrender to Divine Will, your Highest Self, your Most Fully Conscious and Enlightened Self, or whatever other label you ascribe to what I am referring to. If you have never surrendered in this way and asked for ever-increasing discernment and faith, I recommend that you do it right now. If you have already done so, I recommend that you do it right now. If you have already done so a thousand times, I recommend that you do it right now.

We begin both the introduction and commentary with the most important thing. Individuals who are on a spiritual path but who have not yet surrendered to their Highest Self are missing a very important point, and to a great degree, they are at risk of falling into the greatest pitfall of all—falling prey to what I call The Great Deception.

The Great Deception is falling into the trap of Do What Thy Will, as opposed to following the enlightened path of Thy Will Be Done. "Thy Will" in the latter case is not the will of the personified Christian God as the Biblical reference might suggest, but rather, the will of your Highest Self... which is, of course, Divine Will, and is, in fact, the will of the actual Christian God, the One underneath all the misconceptions and misunderstandings. His/Her will IS that we are aligned with and expressing our Highest Self at all times. What Would Jesus Do? He would continue to surrender ever more deeply to his Highest Self in every moment.

Do What Thy Will is a phrase that was popularized in modern times by the famous occultist Aleister Crowley, well known for his involvement in black magic, ritual magic, and some very dark activities. Do What Thy Will was clearly at play in the teachings and actions of Osho, the greatest false light and false prophet of the 20th century, a singular, very gifted, but misguided individual who has led millions and millions of seekers astray[20]. Do What Thy Will even creeps into the teachings of Deepak Chopra in a subtle way when he tells us that we are perfect as we are by invoking the analogy that the baby who cannot yet walk is still perfect, when he tells us that all of our desires will lead us to the face of God. It seems to me that even some number of Tibetan Rinpoches, individuals who are widely considered within their faith to be fully enlightened masters... It seems to me that even some number of, or perhaps many of these highly regarded spiritual teachers have fallen into this trap as well, using their notion of "breaking concepts"[21] in order to rationalize any and all behaviors, throwing out the safety mechanism of conventional wisdom and rules, which may indeed block our progress at times, but without a clear compass of surrender to their Highest Self, or what they might label the Buddha Mind. To me it appears a gross omission that so many Buddhist texts and verbal teachings refer to realizing our Buddha Nature, but nowhere have I heard or read the teaching to surrender to our Buddha Nature, a subtle difference but one of paramount importance.

In Osho, we get a hint of the magnitude of perversions that can occur under the false premise that we are all perfect as we are, that even our pathologies are perfect, and that it can serve us to act out our addictions and pathologies as some sort of misguided exercise in surrender or radical acceptance of Self and All That Is. We get a hint of the type of behavior that emanates from The Great Deception and misapplying partial truths in order to rationalize Do What Thy Will behavior. It was at least in part this type of confused thinking and rationalization that led Osho to sanction "Encounter Groups" at his Ashram in India, where individuals would be locked in a room together and free to act out whatever they felt moved to do in the moment – including physical violence and sexual acts – under the misguided premise of healing and spiritual development[22]. It is this same type of confusion and warped rationalization that enabled Osho's most senior disciples who were living with him at the time to somehow rationalize poisoning and killing five people in the small Oregon town neighboring the Osho Ranch in the United States. It is this same misguided thinking – that it can actually serve us and anyone else for us to act out our addictions and pathologies because we are perfect as we are and there is no right or wrong or objective reality and we should just be present with and accept what is (including our own and other peoples' pathological behaviors) – along with any amount of other misguided spiritual nonsense (which does, in fact, become nonsense when we misuse otherwise potentially helpful partial truths, misapplying them out of context in order to justify harmful activities)... It is this same misguided thinking that still plagues many of Osho's disciples and their students to this day, that continues to have a strong influence on the thinking of many modern seekers, as Osho disciples and individuals further down his lineage continue to write books, start or work at spirituality centers, and teach and model their confused notions of the spiritual path and warped morality – often times with their best intentions, themselves confused and not understanding that they are accidentally leading others into perhaps the most damaging and dangerous trap of all, the one they have fallen into and set up camp in for decades. And, it is The Great Deception that has almost entirely infiltrated the world of Western Tantric Sexuality thanks in part to many of the best known teachers being Osho disciples or students of his disciples, making that world a virtual spiritual mine field in which teachers, practitioners and students alike prey upon and encourage other peoples' addictions and pathologies under the false pretense of spiritual awakening and/or sexual healing. In this world, so many people experience false healing experiences, which are often times just a misperceived and misunderstood yet sometimes ecstatic and highly pleasurable experience of flipping from one side of a pathological drama to the other side, from pain to pleasure, from victim to perpetrator, from sexually abused to sexual manipulator – leading them down a path that often centers around the improper generation and use of sexual energy and the power it can produce. There are at least tens of thousands of people lost in the small universe of Tantric Sexuality alone, which to a great extent is just a small subset of Osho's dark web that is plaguing the minds and souls of millions and the broader landscape of modern spirituality.

Of course, this goes back much further than Osho to the Tibetans of a thousand years ago (and indeed goes back to before then too). It could be argued that Osho was just an obscuration in Tilopa's mind stream[23]. I write this with all due respect to Tilopa and the great Tibetan teachers that came before and after him, and I write this with Tilopa's blessing. He is glad that I am clarifying this extremely important blind spot that has been promulgated in his name.

Also in the introduction, there are a number of other important points that may benefit from further development and explanation.

The introduction suggests the existence of an Objective Reality or Reality As It Is, a concept that is not popular today among the relativists/moral relativists that have been dominating the modern spirituality movement for the past 40 years or more. Moral relativism is particularly appealing in as much as it allows us to lose sight of principles, get around notions of right and wrong, and hide our bad actions from our self and others behind the cloak of subjective reality. It is a great way to rationalize acting out addictions or to avoid admitting to bad behavior when someone calls us on it by responding, "I hear you expressing your truth, but that is not my truth." In my experience, many people who are very much into The Secret, books on the Law of Attraction, books by Abraham and/or who often use the phrase "we create our own reality" – in my experience, many of these people are at least somewhat confused and are sometimes very confused about the fundamental nature of our existence and the framework within which we operate. As if it is our perceptual lens that determines the objective reality of the different wavelengths associated with different colors of light. Philosophically, they have failed to realize the self-contradictory nature of the statement, "There are no absolutes." As such, they are confused about the basic construction of reality, and they are bound to take ill-informed actions that lead to unnecessary suffering for themselves and everyone else.

Of course, we do live in a dynamic reality, and our ordinary perception of the external world as solid and fixed and not influenced by our intentions, perceptual lens, and what we are projecting onto the mirror of physical reality is equally in error. It's not that physical reality is an illusion; it's the way we normally view or understand it that is an illusion.

Also with regards to the dynamic nature of reality, the language in the introduction about the light at the end of the tunnel is an oversimplification, or possibly misleading. The light is not a fixed endpoint that we can get to and stay in forever, as if we are finally finished, as if consciousness is done growing and evolving—a process which will, in fact, never end. The light at the end of the tunnel, i.e., enlightenment, is really just an endpoint of this cycle of learning and growth, an elevated plateau, a beautiful moment on the upward spiral that may last 5 minutes, 50 days or 500 years, but which is not permanent, and from which we will inevitably be pulled into the productive confusion that comes as we continue to move up the spiral, embarking on the next phase of development, learning and evolution[24]. It is like the small child standing on the beach 1000 years ago before ships and airplanes could circumnavigate the globe and saying to their parents that the ocean goes forever. From a practical standpoint, from the child's perspective, this is actually true. The child could not possibly swim across the ocean or see what is on the other side, and could only imagine or guess that there might be other lands and civilizations across the infinite sea. There are many such instances throughout the book when I use language that suggests a static endpoint, which is a convenient and useful model for conveying important ideas and aspects of reality, even if it is not a fully accurate depiction.

The incomplete model, the rough approximation of Reality As It Is, is a built in trap that shows up almost everywhere in spiritual teachings and more broadly in how we conceive of reality and make decisions. When we are operating at the level of mind, we cannot possibly process and take into account all of reality—we must simplify to comprehend and formulate strategies. This state of affairs is equally true for individuals developing strategies to achieve happiness, corporations formulating strategies to maximize profits, and government policy makers developing strategies to enhance their national interest or the interests of particular sectors of society. Incomplete mental models are a fact of life, and it is important to constantly double check the appropriateness of a model for a given situation. Models are very useful when used properly and when we don't forget they are just the map, not the territory. I believe the light at the end of the tunnel analogy is a good and useful model in the context of the Introduction, even if it is not entirely accurate. But it is good for us to not take anything for granted.

Commentary on chapter 1

IT IS POSSIBLE to be fully enlightened and incarnate in physical form. A large percentage of people believe the opposite to be true and are wrong about this, including, of course, anyone that buys into Buddhist teachings on this topic. I met a powerfully dark man once who used this fundamental limiting thought pattern—that we can't be pure light in these bodies—to hide his eyes from and stay in his own darkness[25]. To some degree, many people use this delusion—that we're human and can't be perfect in these bodies—to rationalize not bettering themselves and moving forward on the path of progress in important ways.

My first human memory is from a past life I would place approximately 25,000 years ago. In that life, I was fully enlightened for that stage of human development and biological evolution. I had a perfectly clear, yet primitive mind. I had no karma. It was a good life. I had a mate and three children. We lived in a tropical climate, and I bathed in a lagoon. There were no other people around. At all. To the best of my recollection, I did not have any regular contact with any other humans outside of my immediate family for that entire life time. I was an early human, before there were many of us on the planet. I had no karma. I believed in a higher power and revered the Creator, and as such, I was fully human, not some other less developed humanoid mammal. I knew that I was made from the same stuff as the plants and that the Creator was in all of us. I thanked God for my food before I ate.

I, myself, did not even believe in past lives as recently as three years ago, when I began having past life memories. I was having profound experiences on a regular basis remembering key aspects of past lives—typically the most traumatic memories that had imprinted on my soul and needed to be accessed to clear out the related karmic imprints—but my mind still did not entirely accept that these were actually my past lives. Perhaps they were traumatic memories stored in the collective consciousness that somehow I was accessing, or perhaps these experiences were in some way associated with me and my consciousness, but not actually memories from lifetimes my soul had lived before. Singular memories from a past life would open a doorway into that life, and once that doorway was open, often times more memories would come through, and/or I would be able to feel more deeply into the emotional experience, state of being, and journey of that entire lifetime. Over a period of two and a half years, I got well acquainted with five consecutive past lives spanning back almost a thousand years, in addition to having other important remembrances from a number of other lifetimes, some of which are still less easy to place in the chronological development of my soul. Looking back through my most recent five lives as well as my current life, it is crystal

Reinventing Truth

clear to me that all of them are the life and unfolding of one soul. Just as a self-aware person can look back and examine their life and see patterns and themes, so too, can I look back across these lifetimes and see similar patterns and themes. More so, I have had some of the same people show up across life times, as well. Many of my family members and other important players in my current life played important roles in lives past, as well. Subjectively, I experience continuity of my own consciousness and sense of self across these life times. I experience these lifetimes as the rising and falling of the human form with me, the constant observer, there throughout, in a similar way I experienced the rising and falling of my abdomen with each breath while sitting in a monastery a number of years ago, with me, the constant observer, there throughout. Very recently, I had an experience in which I was talking to a friend about the veil between lives being lifted, and right at that moment, I felt one of my past lives come through in an intense way that is difficult to describe. I felt his feelings and the experience of being him in a way that was 10 times stronger or more than I had ever felt before—as if I was actually him in that moment. I experienced a type of buzzing in my head and couldn't see straight, and I was filled with intense anger. My friend told me that she couldn't be 100% sure what she saw, but it appeared to her that my face had actually changed—my eyes sinking more deeply into my skull and becoming darker, and the bridge of my nose becoming wider. Her report rang true to me as not only possible but also consistent with my experience of that unusual 30 seconds.

Parsimony, also called Ockham's razor, is a principle often applied in scientific settings that states that the simplest theory that accounts for all the data is the accurate theory, even if there are other, more complex competing theories that also account for all the data. The initial theories I developed to account for my past life memories are more complex than the basic theory of past lives and reincarnation, and in fact, they don't really account for all of the data anyway (e.g., family members and other individuals showing up across these life times). For me, it has become increasingly clear over time that my past life memories are just that—memories from past lives my soul has lived. Not only is that my subjective experience, but also, I can come up with no clearer, simpler, more reasonable explanation for my experiences, as well as how all of these experiences fit into my broader, internally coherent and fully integrated process of healing and awakening. Past lives are real.

With regards to the central content of Chapter 1, many students of modern spirituality may struggle with the notion that things can actually go wrong, and the obvious corollary that we can make mistakes. Many students of modern spirituality believe that we are all God and that God is in everything and that everything is a perfect expression of God and part of the Divine Plan. Many spiritual teachers and writers believe these things to be true as well.

Since we have free will—which we do—we are given the choice in each moment of how we want to direct our energy and intention in this physical realm. We are given the choice to fully express our Highest Self or to chase pleasurable experiences or to let dark programs run us, to let other consciousnesses or thought forms take over our thoughts, speech and actions. It is certainly a mistake and not part of the Divine Plan when we choose a dark path, when in fact, we choose anything but expressing our Highest Self.

The organizing intelligence of the universe is so awesome, that no matter what we choose in each moment, in the very next moment, everything is already set up to give us a path from where we are to experiencing the bliss of full enlightenment. Reality reconfigures around us in each moment, opening a new door for us to step through towards the Light, orchestrating a new set of synchronicities to lead us there. At any point in time we can look back on our life path and see how everything was set up to lead us to exactly where we are, and this is true no matter how many mistakes we have made and how many times we have strayed from the path of surrender to our Highest Self. Because this is true, it is easy for us to think that we were always on the path and never strayed from it. It is easy for us to get confused and think that we never made any mistakes and that everything including our wrong action was part of the perfect, Divine Plan[26].

As God Sparks we are expressions of God, but this does not mean we are always choosing and bringing light in. It just means we have consciousness and can make choices—nothing more. Confusing the Christian God—which we naturally think of as good and light—with the basic building blocks of reality and pure consciousness—which can be used to bring in more light or more darkness—can lead us into some basic mental traps on this point.

I first broke out of this mental trap myself roughly six years ago, which very quickly led me to experience parallel realities and gain the benefits of integrating parallel lives – the first occurrences in my personal development process which form the basis of this chapter. More recently, I had an interesting experience in which for several days I was in regular mental contact with a parallel version of myself who was living in a different house in the same town I live in right now. I was supposed to live in that house, but something went wrong, and someone else is living there now. When I went into and began processing the karmic wound that led to this chain of events that kept me out of the house I was supposed to be in, all of a sudden this parallel me popped in, and I could experience the peace and satisfaction of being grounded in that wonderful home. I have had some significant blocks around putting down roots and finding a home for myself throughout my life, and this parallel version of me had already worked through these specific blocks as demonstrated by the fact that he had found a home in which he felt centered and grounded, a home where he belonged. Over a period of several days, this parallel self essentially downloaded to me the experience of being healed in that way, and as a result, I, in this time line, found another home and broke through the old blockades holding me back in this area of my life. This other home, the one I am sitting in right now as I type, came into my life in a very synchronous way that also brought other benefits with it, i.e., things I might call silver linings if I didn't know better. What was further interesting about all of this, after I moved into my current home, I realized that the parallel me living in that other house was holding some different emotional wounds that either 1) I had had to work through in this time line in order to move into

Reinventing Truth

my new home or 2) will naturally fall away as a result of me living in this house instead of that one. When I saw his unresolved issues, I sent him a great deal of compassion and essentially downloaded to him the experience of being healed in these other places, completing a mutually beneficial exchange between these parallel selves. Finally, a couple weeks later, I spoke with the individual involved in the karmic episode in which that person unconsciously contributed to blocking me from moving into the home I was meant to live in. We both had a good cry and learned from the episode, at which time the parallel me integrated back into me.

Commentary on chapter 2

How many of you got carried away with the new toy I gave you in Chapter 1 and let its shininess crowd out the rest of your field of vision? How many of you overcompensated and concluded that every painful event in your life is actually something that went wrong?

How many of you thought of a military battle or other violent analogy when picturing you or someone else with their bare feet and hands in the dirt, battling for good? Why is it that our first thought isn't of someone planting trees?

Commentary on chapter 3

EMBRACING PARADOX AND being equally comfortable in either side of a given paradox is a wonderful thing because it gives us freedom of action—it does not allow our partial understanding of reality to limit us from taking actions inconsistent with the side of the paradox we are stuck in. It gives us a mental rationalization for either choice—for going left or right at the fork in the road. When our minds can justify going in either direction, we are more free to follow intuition, follow our discernment, the inner voice which is our Highest Self telling us which way to go. If we only believe in a dualistic reality filled with good and evil, it will be difficult for us to follow the inner voice and do nothing, and accept the bad around us in any given moment. If we only believe in a non-dual reality with no right and wrong, it will be difficult for us to follow the inner voice that is telling us to stand up and fight for what is right, to be a peaceful warrior of light, effecting tangible change in the physical world around us and in the realms of spirit.

When we develop a full range of motion in our consciousness, when we are able to easily and regularly embrace paradox, we are freed from conventional wisdom and culturally popular ways of seeing things. We are freed from the way we have usually seen things. Our mind knows that it alone does not have the answer, which makes more room for our heart and other aspects of our intelligence to shine through, always guided by our Highest Self. Our mind knowing that it alone does not have the answer creates more space for our Highest Self to spontaneously emanate through us with less resistance from a rigid belief system.

Of course, some people get too carried away with this and think that having any belief systems at all is a negative thing or a barrier. They think that the mind is just an obstruction and fail to utilize this powerful tool and intelligence center to its fullest capacity, integrating its wisdom with other centers of intelligence to come to the best possible conclusions, make the best possible choices and take the best possible actions in any given moment. Discarding the value of belief systems and mental reasoning as a whole is also a trap, and one which dark people and non-human consciousnesses alike use to confuse and lead people astray.

Commentary on chapter 4

SPIRITUAL EGOTISM IS a pitfall that very many people fall into at some point on their path. I have been there myself. It is such a dangerous trap because it limits our growth and can keep us stuck in patterns that don't serve us; it can make it more difficult for us to see our blind spots and pathologies, to see where we still have much work to do. When lost in spiritual egotism, we become the full teacup into which no more teachings can be poured. We lose beginners mind. Our garden still has many weeds, yet through our distorted lens and having never seen a weedless garden, we think our garden is beautiful, so we let the weeds continue to overgrow the garden. Perhaps we have come so far, the garden is so much more beautiful than it used to be that we think it is actually finished or almost finished.

While many "beginners" fall into spiritual egotism, this specific trap is one that many "advanced" students and long time spiritual seekers get stuck in. In particular, I have found that some portion of spiritual teachers, healers, yoga teachers, and more broadly people who earn money in some sort of healing art or holistic modality can be prone to getting caught in this specific snare.

One reason this happens is because very often these people have psychic abilities and/or unique perceptual abilities. As such, their egos have a tendency to come in and make them think they are special, which on one level is true. But, if their ego is under-developed in any way, they run the risk of equating special with superhuman, above the fray, as if they have everything all figured out. When they observe how their insights positively impact their clients, they get continued reinforcement that they are seeing and experiencing reality clearly and that they are looking at the world through a clear lens. Because part of their lens is so unblemished – the section through which they look at other peoples' issues and wounds, not their own – because of this fact, they are sometimes less able to see the areas where their lens might be a bit cloudy, sometimes less able to turn their vision on themself and see their own wounds and pathologies and blind spots.

Making matters more difficult for spiritual teachers and healers is the fact that often times their livelihood, professional identity & reputation, and a meaningful portion of their self-esteem can be tied up in their spiritual persona[27], making it that much more challenging for people in these fields not to get wrapped up in spiritual egotism to some degree. This does not happen to every teacher and holistic practitioner, of course, but when it does happen, it is unfortunate. When they are operating at the level of spiritual egotism, otherwise highly realized teachers and practitioners are less likely to see their own blind spots, flawed thinking and pathologies, which both limits their own progress and joy, and also makes it that much more likely they will unknowingly pass these unwanted gifts to their students and clients – people who are often impressionable and subject to the natural power imbalance that occurs between doctor and patient, teacher and student.

To those of you reading who are spiritual teachers or who practice the healing arts, please remember to maintain beginner's mind and not to assume that you are further along the path than you actually are. Your special gifts and calling in life have put you in a position where your level of development has a disproportionate impact on the lives and spiritual development of others. Whether you or they realize it or not, your pathologies and mental viruses are often times directly downloaded into your clients along with the light and love and support that you bring. This is happening between all of us all the time to some degree, but in my experience, it happens to a much greater degree in the specific context of spiritual teaching and healing work.

Commentary on chapter 5

ANOTHER COMMON MISUNDERSTANDING about karma is the notion of karmic debt. Many people believe that we have karmic debts that must be paid. Many people believe that they must live through and bear the difficult aspects of their lives as conscious penance for their past sins, in order to pay off their karmic debt. People stuck in this limiting belief system are enduring way more pain and suffering than they need to and are unwittingly slowing their progress to full enlightenment.

It's not as if we borrow money from the bank we must pay back. In each and every moment some, or perhaps all, of our debts can be forgiven. Not by some external messiah figure, but by our self. The most powerful healing force on the planet is your own compassion. Developing compassion and directing it inward to our own wounds can instantaneously heal these wounds, instantaneously clear our karma, forgive our karmic debts. Self forgiveness, forgiving our own karmic debts, sending our self compassion. These are all the same thing, and none of them require the intervention of Jesus or God forgiving our sins, or a spiritual guru showing us the path. We can learn to do this our self, first learning to shine the light of our compassion to very specific wounds, very specific and small pieces of karma, and over time building the strength and expanse of our light so that we can clear out bigger and bigger chunks, whole lifetimes of karma in a single sitting. Our efforts can be supported by Jesus or God or a spiritual teacher or a friend, but they are our own efforts. We have this ability innate within us and it is wise to make a point of developing this ability for our own benefit and the benefit of all sentient beings.

Commentary on chapter 6

BUDDHISM AVOIDS THE existence of souls because souls represent the reification of self, a form of essentialism, in which the essence of our Self, our soul, remains in tact as a distinct form that we can identify with across lifetimes and the unfolding and development of consciousness in the physical realm. As such, souls come with all sorts of problems, in fact, many of the same problems we associate with separation and having an ego.

The Buddha lived in India at a time when Vedic Brahmanism (essentially an early form of Hinduism) was the dominant religion/philosophy, and like other famous spiritual teachers and prophets, the Buddha became famous because he had insights that added to and/or contradicted the mainstream beliefs of his time and place, added to and/or contradicted the predominant culture and spiritual tradition he grew up in.

Hindus, like the Vedic Brahmans, believe in souls and reincarnation.

The Hindu experience of reality is that we are particles. The Buddhist experience of reality is that we are not particles, we are waves. According to Buddhist teachings, all phenomena including us arise from causes and conditions. All phenomena are empty, which means that nothing has any innate characteristics. Nothing is solid. It's as if a boulder is dropped into one side of the pond and another boulder is dropped into the other side of the pond, and in the middle of the pond as a result of the interaction of the ripples moving across the pond, a spherical drop of water rises above the pond for just a brief moment. That drop is you. You are the result of causes and conditions.

The Buddha was right. As were the Hindus. Each religion embraces one side of the paradox. The Truth is we are both a particle and a wave.

When studying physics in high school and college, I always struggled with getting my mind around how light could both be a particle and a wave at the same time and how it could behave as one or the other depending on the circumstances. To this day I still do not have the proper words or mental conceptualization to resolve this fundamental paradox that is so central to the nature of Reality and All That Is. However, I have had direct experience in a monastery of experiencing being both a particle and a wave simultaneously. Being solid and not solid simultaneously. My direct experience of this reality gave me something that is beyond what can be contained in my mind's language center, beyond what I can distill down into words.

Interestingly, the Tibetans stray from the Theravada tradition significantly, bending towards the notion of souls without actually fully crossing over to the other side of the

Reinventing Truth

paradox. Their practical experience of having various gurus, including the Dali Lama, continue to reincarnate again and again, could not be explained by the traditional Buddhist paradigm, so they had to modify their teachings to conform to their observed reality. A casual student of Tibetan Buddhism might believe that the Tibetans believe in souls and reincarnation just like the Hindus; whereas they technically do not. The Tibetan gurus finesse the point with a slight of hand, indicating that a well-developed mind stream can generate enough psychic force to keep continuity and flow across human lives, similar to a soul. They stick to the analogy of a stream, since it is not solid, and it helps them avoid reification of the Self, a fundamental tenet of Buddhism.

In this example, we see how belief systems that subscribe to a partial truth, to one side of a given paradox, in one way or another will bump up against Reality As It Is, and will be unable to reconcile certain data points. Which, on a side note, is one more example of where we do not "create our own reality". Just because we embrace a partial truth does not mean that things wont eventually enter or force their way into our field that don't fit our incomplete worldview. On the contrary, reality is set up so that we will eventually know the whole Truth, so it is inevitable that events and situations will poke into our reality that do not fit our flawed and/or incomplete paradigms. These are the opportunities for growth and evolution of consciousness.

It is no coincidence that the roots of Hinduism and Buddhism are intertwined and that specifically Tibetan Buddhism more directly draws from Hinduism and in some ways bridges the two faiths, embracing both sides of the paradox to some degree, while still largely occupying one side of the paradox, siding with the Buddha.

That said, I read somewhere that the Buddha himself would not answer when he was asked if we had souls. It could be that the Buddha fully realized the paradox, which is why he would not answer yes or no to a question that can't be answered that way. If this is true, then the Buddhist teachings in my mind represent the best efforts of his disciples and other great minds in his lineage to codify his teachings to the best of their abilities and based on their less than full realization of what he was conveying to them. It seems almost inevitable that religions promulgated by less realized individuals than the originating founder will contain many distortions of the original teachings, including some distortions which are very important indeed. This is no doubt the case with Christianity and could very well be true of Buddhism as well. Back then, neither the Buddha nor his followers had the benefit of modern knowledge of quantum physics and the basic reality that light is both a particle and wave at the same time. Even assuming the Buddha got this paradox 2500 years before science would be able to observe it in physical reality, it seems clear that his students and the great Buddhist writers and teachers since that time largely did not.

And, truth be told, while I raise the possibility that the Buddha got the paradox, and while I would like to give him the benefit of the doubt, my actual belief is that he only got one side of the paradox. My actual belief is he got as far as possible into the new side of the paradox, explored the most distant and remote frontiers of the new side of the paradox, the one he and others had been missing before...

so much so, that he got confused and thought that a compelling part of the dream was actually the fullness of reality. No doubt the depth and degree of the pioneering journey he took in order to map that aspect of reality for us and direct us with regards to how to experience it for our self, as well as the volumes of other powerfully positive and essential insights and teachings he shared with us – no doubt these achievements place the Buddha as an incredibly significant historical figure and light bearer; however, with regards to this particular paradox, my belief is that he only got part of the story right, not the whole thing.

Commentary on chapter 7

THE EGO IS a construct that creates borders between Self and everything else, enabling us to function in differentiated physical reality. God is boundless. Identifying with God is an oxymoron, since God is beyond what is possible to be wrapped in an ego, necessary for identification to occur. People who identify with God or the Source are confused, and are likely to fall into any number of other mental traps, leading to needless suffering for themselves and others.

Seeing that well-known spiritual teachers have made this mistake is a good reminder that they too are human and flawed. It is important as we develop that we take more and more of our power back, that we see teachers as people who may have some interesting partial realizations that we can benefit from but who do not "have it all figured out". It is important that we don't hand our self over to them entirely, or accept their version of reality as true without testing it out for our self, thinking critically about it, feeling into our body with it, and the likes. Just as there is a growing awareness in certain circles that we shouldn't give our power away to doctors and listen to everything they tell us because they are working within one limited paradigm, it is similarly important that we be our own general practitioners of spirit, treating spiritual teachers and healers as specialists that we manage, not allowing them to think for us, not taking all of the spiritual antidotes they prescribe without doing our own research first. Some of these antidotes may be bad for us altogether; some may do more harm than good; while others may be generally good for us while having some small side effects we can overcome as we add our fuller conception of Truth to the specific remedy they prescribe.

Commentary on chapter 8

SIMILAR TO THE light at the end of the tunnel in the introduction, the perfect YOU inside is not a static endpoint. The perfect YOU is the fully enlightened version of you at the end of this cycle of your soul's development of human development. This does not mean your soul will not continue to evolve after you achieve this level of perfection. It will. This level of perfection is perfection from our current vantage point, just like the ocean that goes on forever for the young child standing on the beach 1000 years ago. It is not actually the final end point, since there is no such thing.

If you have not already done so, at some point on your journey, you will very likely become aware of and intimately connected with this consciousness that is the fully enlightened future you. The first time I had this experience was in 2003, and at the time I did not realize that the immensely compassionate and loving heart I was encountering was in fact, my own. Based on my Christian upbringing the only thing that fit my mental model at the time was that this must be the heart of Jesus. For about two years I was convinced that I had had a direct experience of connecting with Jesus' heart, when in fact, I had actually experienced connecting with the heart of future me. I did not have the right mental model at the time to accurately make sense of the experience. Over time, I was less sure of what that experience was, and it wasn't until I was sitting by myself eating lunch in Austin, Texas near the end of 2007 or the beginning of 2008 that I had a very clear encounter with my future self. I was in a difficult moment sitting with some difficult feelings when all of a sudden I felt waves of warm, loving energy caressing my face. After being with this physical sensation for a few seconds, I became distinctly aware that the source of this energy was, in fact, my future self sending love and compassion and support back in time to me from the future. At this point in my development I had already experienced backwards causation in time and any number of other mind bending and consciousness expanding experiences, and I had spent upwards of 100 hours or more sending compassion back in time to past versions of myself in this lifetime and lifetimes past as part of the process of healing and integrating my wounded fragments and clearing out heaps of karma. By this time, I had enough accumulated experiences to make better sense of the reality that was coming in at that moment, and it was a really beautiful thing to sit and be bathed in the love and compassion that I was sending back to myself. I could feel the heart that was emanating that compassion back to me—i.e., my future heart—and it was a comforting and profoundly healing experience to know that someday that beautiful, powerful and deeply compassionate and loving heart would be my heart.

Since that time, I have had regular contact with my future self, and I have also connected with the fully enlightened future self of one other person. That too was a wonderful experience, which was especially encouraging for me because this individual at the time was very wounded and being run by some addictions and dark programs. Connecting with and catching a glimpse of this person's fully enlightened future self gave me tremendous hope for humankind and deepened my trust in this process of unfoldment towards enlightenment that we are all going through. To see that she would get from where she was at that moment to becoming the beautifully powerful light being I encountered, was an inspiring experience that continues to illuminate the way I view people I come into contact with on a day-to-day basis.

Commentary on chapter 9

PEOPLE WHO DON'T understand Divine Will may be confused when they see you running into difficulty in your life, may say that you aren't following Divine Will but are just confused and following your addictions and pathologies into traps, burning off your karma the most difficult way, by living through tough experiences in the physical realm. When you hear these voices, it is important to dig a little deeper and be that much more clear in your discernment, that much more sure that you are surrendered to your Highest Self. It is important not to become defensive. They may have important information for you.

At the same time, you must understand that following your Divine Path may be difficult at times. Each person's path is different and unique. Sometimes Divine Will for your life is to transform your karma via spiritual practice and through meditation. Other times, Divine Will for your life is for you to become aware of and work through your karma by seeing your wounds and karmic patterns reflected back at you in the mirror of physical reality. Many spiritual teachers and spiritual people have a bias in favor of spiritual practice as the best or only path to purification and enlightenment, and as a result, they are discounting the value of living a full life in the physical world and using the difficult events in life as doorways to go deeper into spiritual awakening, as opportunities to see and powerfully clear karmic patterns once and for all.

Five life times ago, I was a well-known Buddhist teacher who meditated for many years in caves. The people around me said that I was fully enlightened and would not have to reincarnate again as a result of my spiritual practice and realizations in that lifetime. Buddhists to this day believe that this man, Milarepa, was a fully enlightened master that would not come back again in human form. Not only did I come back, but also, much of the worst and deepest karma I have had to clear since that time emanates from and/or was deepened in that lifetime. Many years meditating in caves did not clear the bad karma I created for myself in that lifetime and in the lifetimes before. It had tremendous benefit for sure, but it did not clear my karma.

Furthermore, my spiritual pursuits and efforts to dissolve out my ego, created a spring back effect in my following life. In my next life, I was an extremely powerful and controlling man driven by my wounded ego. My ego had had enough of passively surrendering to physical reality and being suppressed and restrained and hated—so in the next life, my ego came back with a vengeance so to speak, behaving as a wild beast that had just been let out of a cage after being tortured for far too long. I speak from my own experience, the experience of my soul's progression, when I say that ego suppression and over-immersion in spirit realms may or may not be a good thing. In my lifetime

Reinventing Truth

as Milarepa, I was following a mental model, a prescription that was based on a certain belief system, and one that did not include the concept of surrendering to Divine Will or the Buddha Mind, one that did not hold a sacred space for a fully healed and integrated ego. I followed the recipe and got a lot of good results, but this does not mean I was on my Divine Path. It means I had a lot of mental discipline and a lot of faith in my teacher, perhaps more faith in him than in myself, seeing as I could not trust my own judgment and impulses following the major missteps I took early in life.

I did quite a bit of session work with an individual who spent his last 13 consecutive past lives as a Buddhist Monk, the last one of which ended with him being tortured to death in a prison. One of his greatest challenges in this life is to develop a healthy ego. He is highly psychic in part because he has almost no ego, no separation between himself and others. Telepathic communication comes easily to him, as does working with entities and entering into other peoples' energy fields and minds. At the same time, he has great difficulty being around people in many cases because he is so sensitive to any disturbances in their minds or in their energy field—he experiences their disturbances as his own. It's as if when someone walks by wearing a headset listening to music, he experiences music blasting in his head at a painful volume. He has had a challenging life, and quite a bit of our work centered around helping him feel safe reconstructing his ego. Somewhere further back in the life of his soul, he did some very bad things driven by his wounded ego, so he convinced himself and was convinced by his spiritual teachers to dissolve out his ego, to suppress his ego, to transcend his ego so he could achieve enlightenment. He and they may not have realized that a fully functioning and healthy ego is an essential part of an enlightened being.

Commentary on chapter 10

Should the yin/yang symbol actually have a yin/yang in each dot on each side instead of a white dot on the black side and a black dot on the white side?

What would the best possible symbol be to capture the more complex truth that reality is both dual and non-dual at the same time?

Commentary on chapter 11

WE MUST BE very careful with this. It may feel that power is authentically calling to us, when really it is appealing to wounded aspects of our ego that want to feel important or validated in some way, as if we are worth something or our life has had some meaning because of the good we were able to do in the world with the worldly power we accumulated. The desire to do good in the world is one of the most often used rationalizations to justify the quest for power[28]. It is very often a form of self-delusion, a massive blind spot that will be painfully revealed to us and everyone else as time and causation unfolds. It is extremely important that we are especially careful with this one.

One safeguard against this and other potential blind spots is taking care to develop a positive spiritual network and to be very selective in who we spend our time with, who we connect with emotionally, who our friends are, and who we work with or do business with (and of course, who we trust to be our spiritual teachers and healing facilitators). Perhaps you have noticed that one of the most common bonds between friends is one of shared addictions and pathological thought patterns. People who smoke most often are friends with other people who smoke. The same is true of people who drink. The same is true for people who have any number of negative or pathological thought patterns. Mental diseases are contagious. Not necessarily the kinds that western medicine would identify as a disease. What I am referring to are things like the mental disease of objectifying people and seeing them as a means to an end and forgetting that they are fully human. This type of mental disease easily spreads from individuals who have this belief system to other individuals who have the emotional wounding and/or character flaws that would make them susceptible to this type of thinking, this specific mental disease. The clearer we get in our systems and in our thinking, the more time we can spend with people without catching their mental diseases—because we are no longer susceptible to it. But, when we are on our path, when we are still beginners—which all but a very few people are, and let's just assume that you and I both are—when we are still beginners, it is important for us to find and surround our self with people who are at a high vibration and who do not share our mental diseases. It is important for us to be aware that sometimes the people we most like to spend time with are those that are the worst for us. We must develop discernment and become aware of what it is about this other person that we enjoy, what it is about this other person that gives us a charge. We might see that we like them because they reinforce some of our negative beliefs, or we enjoy indulging addictions with them, engaging in activities like drinking and womanizing, or purchasing shoes we can't afford. It may be wise for us to take a small step back from these relationships and seek out relationships with people who are different than the ones we are normally attracted to, people who don't drink or who don't wear expensive shoes.

Furthermore, it is important we find individuals who are loving and supportive friends who have enough insight and who we can trust enough to let them hold a mirror up to us sometimes, even and especially when we might not want to hear what they are telling us. It is these friends that can tell us we are chasing power for the wrong reasons. It is these friends that can help us see maybe we have some issues with our self-esteem, or that we are chasing power so we can have a greater sense of security or control in our lives (and that this very well may be a false sense of security and control). It is these friends that might remind us that we can do good right now, even before we have power, and who might tell us that we are lying to our self if we think we are going to do more good tomorrow than we are doing today.

Commentary on chapter 12

JUST AS IT is important that you do not let others manipulate you in this way, it is important that you no longer manipulate others in this way. Sometimes their negative feelings are totally unfounded, and other times they are an opportunity for you to see some difficult things about yourself in the mirror. Don't miss out on these opportunities for growth and development. Don't put it all back on them, unless it is actually all theirs. Each relationship and each situation has its own proper balance. Finding this balance is an art that takes practice. You will get better at this over time. I promise. And this is true, even if you think you are already a master in this area. There is always another level and a deeper lesson, even when we are blind to it.

Commentary on chapter 13

THIS IS MY favorite chapter. I hope you will read it again.

It has only been during the last year or so when I have awakened to the level where I can easily become conscious of other peoples' programs running me. I have literally had experiences of thinking thoughts and realizing that they were not my thoughts but coming from the outside as part of someone else's script. Feeling feelings and realizing that they were not my feelings but coming from the outside as part of someone else's script. I have experienced people accidentally and in at least one case intentionally putting thoughts into my head, thoughts that I may have perceived as my own had I not developed a finer level of discernment over the years as a result of all the meditation and healing work that I have done, as a result of doing quite a bit of work specifically with several highly realized, highly psychic individuals who helped me tap into and develop previously underutilized parts of my mind.

I am fortunate in that I have received many empowerments from several Tibetan Rinpoches, including the Mahakala empowerment, one of the protector deities of the Drikung Kagyu lineage of Tibetan Buddhism. By saying the Mahakala Mantra I am able to instantaneously block out any and all external programs that might otherwise be penetrating into my field and mind stream without my knowledge. Saying this mantra essentially puts up a powerful psychic shield. For those of you wanting to take greater control of your life in this specific way, I highly recommend finding a tool that is suitable for you to accomplish this same task. Besides protector deities and psychic shields, I know some people seem to benefit from talismans or the recent fad of wearing pendants with copper wire wrapped inside. I have not worn one of these myself or even tried one on, but I get the sense that they do amplify your own energy field and help keep out to some degree other peoples' scripts and other external thought forms, energy and the likes. I would not rely entirely on a physical artifact, since it can be disempowering to place our power in an object, but perhaps it can be part of the solution for some people for some period of time.

In addition to experiencing thoughts come into my head from the outside, I also had a waking vision of a dark tractor beam coming out of some one's field and pulling me down in spite of my greatest efforts to spread my angel wings and fly. In this instance, it appeared that the only way I could break free and fly was to put some significant distance between me and this individual—physically, emotionally and psychically.

Waking up to these more subtle yet very important layers of reality can have some very real and sometimes difficult implications for our lives. It may result in you re-

Reinventing Truth

alizing you need to end long-standing, previously important friendships. It may lead you to distance yourself from certain members of your family or quite possibly to end your marriage. Or these realizations may lead you to quit your job if you become aware of the darkness in the mind stream of the organization you are working for[29]. In case you were not already aware of it, organizations very much have consciousness too, and their consciousnesses are separate from yet related to the consciousnesses of their individual members. In the awakening that is happening today on earth, it is important that we not only draw forth our Highest Self and help others do the same, but also draw forth the Highest Self of the organizations we are involved with, including the large corporations which are some of the most powerful volitional consciousnesses alive on the planet today.

At some point in our process our light will be so strong that we don't have to escape the dark tractor beam, we can stay in it and shine our light so brightly that the tractor beam melts away and the other individual is transformed while in our presence, so THEY must choose either to stay and embrace the light or run away if they want to stay in their darkness[30]—or rather if their darkness has such a hold of them that it will compel them to run away before their true Self has a chance to make the life giving choice. And, even while this is true, even while at some point our light will be this strong, it is important we not overestimate where we are in the process. This is another situation in which the trap of spiritual egotism can be extremely dangerous. We might think we are stronger than we are, want to believe that we are more developed than we actually are, that we can actually help someone else out of their darkness that is also pulling us down. It requires a great level of discernment to determine when it is wise to run into the burning building to save a loved one, when it is wise to jump into the quicksand to pull someone else out. If we are lacking in self-esteem, we are more likely to put our self in harm's way so we can feel good about our self and the contribution we are trying to make in other peoples' lives. We must be very careful with trying to be a hero. Sometimes the most difficult and heroic thing we can do is to save our self. Other times, we can put out the fire with our presence, transform the quicksand into a stairway out of a difficult situation, transform the flying daggers into daisies. This is just one more example of why it is so important to ask for and continue to develop ever-increasing, ever-accurate discernment.

Discernment is one of the benefits of meditation, and specifically doing a 10 day or longer Vipassana meditation retreat. Our discernment is greatly enhanced by the ability to move out of ordinary awareness, which is often engaged in the drama of a given situation, and move into the clarity of observational mind. Furthermore, meditation and Vipassana meditation in particular, may prove very useful in helping us get in touch with and know our self, so that we can get clearer on the baseline reality of who we are when we are not interacting with all the normal characters in our life. Most of us probably do not realize how malleable we are, to what extent different people bring out different aspects of us, including aspects that we don't like or would rather not act out. Taking some time away from our ordinary life in directed meditation can shed a lot of light on this aspect of reality once we return to our ordinary life with a heightened awareness and paying special attention to which parts of our self other people draw forth.

It was when reading Deepak Chopra's book <u>How to Know God</u>, when I was first exposed to the idea that our brains are transmitters and receivers. Today that is part of my ordinary direct perception of reality—it is not a theory or a possibility, but the way things really work based on my own personal experience and corroborated by the experience of several individuals I know. In this reality of transmitters and receivers, in a reality where our brains are both transmitting and receiving thought forms and programs all of the time, and doing so with or without our awareness that this is happening… operating with knowledge of these aspects of consciousness and how our minds function, the question of who is creating your reality takes on some new dimensions. The question of where the scripts that are running you come from, where the thoughts in your head that you think are your own thoughts actually come from—these questions take on some new dimensions, as well.

My experience is that we are all co-creating our shared reality all the time, but we are all not equals in this endeavor. Some minds are stronger than others. Some people are more powerful than others. It's as if each of us is a planet or a moon with a gravitational field, and some of us have more mass and gravity than others. We each sit at the center of our own reality, our own vortex so to speak, but our vortex does not encompass the entire universe, and sometimes our course and our vortex can be altered dramatically by someone else who enters our field. Likewise, we can exert quite a bit of gravity on others when we enter their field, as well—depending on our relative mass, the relative strengths of our gravitational fields, our relative levels of power. In this regard, perhaps a historical figure such as the Buddha was a bright star, like the sun, and of course, it is very important we don't get too close to a black hole.

How strong is your mind? Is your gravitational field drawing others towards or away from the Light?

Commentary on chapter 14

PLEASE UNDERSTAND THAT much of what I write in this chapter not only applies to spiritual teachers but also applies to role models in other parts of our lives—mentors, colleagues, coaches, leaders in our field, or other people who we admire or who help us develop some aspect of our self in some way.

If you are a business person, for example, you could re-read this chapter keeping in mind your most important and/or cherished role model—whether it be Richard Branson, Bill Gates, the CEO of your company, or the founder of an innovative socially and environmentally responsible business. You can become conscious of why you admire this person, at which level which aspects of their behavior hook into you. Is it ego-driven? Are they hooking into your old desires of achieving status and power coming from a wounded place, or are they showing you what you might be able to achieve if you surrender to your Highest Self, fully trusting wherever that may take you, even if it is away from the glamor and the power and the money and towards smaller scale, simpler, yet more aligned projects and professional pursuits? You may find that your role models reflect already the positive changes you have made and the depth of your proper internal alignment, or you may realize you need to find some new role models that can better help guide you forward on your path of progress, instead of pulling you back to where you have always wanted to go for many of the wrong reasons.

I have a friend who likes to drink and smoke and go dancing a lot. She raves about a healer who drinks coffee and smokes cigarettes during his healing sessions. She explains how he examines you, smoking cigarettes and drinking coffee while watching you and talking to you for about an hour, before doing some intense body work and energetic work that addresses whatever might need addressing. The excitement about which she specifically mentions the fact he drinks coffee and smokes is fairly telling. It stems from the fact that she has a role model that gives her permission to stay in her addictions. She can fall back on the rationalization of the stories of the great Indian masters who can drink hydrochloric acid without hurting themselves. She can tell herself that we can become powerful enough to transform whatever we put in our body, which means that what we put into our body is not that important, which means it's ok for her to enjoy smoking and drinking without giving it a second thought, as if these behaviors are not bad for her body and spirit. She is excited about this man because his behavior gives her permission to stay in her addictions, never having to look at them. And because he will give her a clean bill of health, never addressing her addictions with her and encouraging her to take on the challenge of breaking free of them. She admires his dark spots as much as his light, because it makes her feel OK about not addressing her own corresponding dark spots.

I believe this dynamic is part of why so many of Osho's students get so defensive and feel threatened when he is criticized. Osho's behavior and teachings have given them permission to stay in and act out all of their addictions and pathologies under the cover of spiritual awakening, surrender and radical acceptance. Many of these people don't want to let go of their addictions and pathologies, or their addictions and pathologies don't want to let go of them—depending on how you look at it. Osho is hooked into their wounds at a fundamentally deep level, and challenging Osho challenges their way of life and their identity. The challenge to their identity can be particularly intense, since many of his disciples go by their Osho name in their professional and personal lives (which to me is another spiritual oxymoron, another pitfall on the spiritual path, building up so much identity around a spiritual name and spiritual teacher – another powerful layer to the Osho trap in particular and a broader trap to be avoided in other circumstances, as well). Challenging Osho then, strikes terror into many of his followers at a deep level, since they are not willing and/or ready to move out of delusion and into reality on some important fronts in life. They don't want to see the sex addiction, the love addiction, the bliss addiction, their self-centeredness, their manipulative tendencies, their confusion they have been passing on to others.

He told us we can have our drugs, sex and rock and roll and do anything we want and still be enlightened people, that following Do What Thy Will is actually the path of enlightenment. What if this isn't true? What if meaningful portions of my life are built on a lie, on a great deception?

It can be extremely frightening to realize that we have been on a false path, that we have been following a false prophet, that we are totally lost and heading with our friends, loved ones, and professional associates in tow in exactly the opposite direction from the Light. The further one goes with a dark teacher and/or down a false path, the more difficult it is to unwind the false reality, the confusion in their minds, and the tangled web of their lives. Knowing all of this, we can be extra careful then in our own lives to choose our role models carefully. To choose our teachers and mentors carefully, whether they be spiritual, professional or personal. And, we can take extra care to check in periodically and make sure the path we are on is true, that we are not inadvertently building our spiritual and material lives on a shaky foundation, or worse yet on quick sand that is slowly pulling us down without our knowledge into dark places we don't want to go.

Commentary on chapter 15

I WROTE THIS chapter with the Tibetans in mind, though it has application to other peoples and spiritual traditions. Cultures, value systems, rights of passage and shared belief systems grow up around religious and spiritual traditions just as they do around economic systems and political groupings. Many of the eastern spiritual traditions value spirit over matter, believe it is more important to sit in a cave and meditate than it is to run for political office or become an environmental activist, more important to achieve and remain in a state of absolute enlightenment, than to see this state of being reflected outward through time and causation into relative, time bound reality. They are helping us go more deeply into the partial truth that most of us have been missing for thousands of years, but they themselves are often times stuck on the other side of the paradox, the more "enlightened" side of the paradox as they might see it.

I have acquaintances that are on 2 year or longer silent retreats in the mountains of Nepal because their Tibetan guru said they should go. In that system, these retreats are a right of passage and assumed as conventional wisdom as something that is beneficial for the serious student seeking enlightenment. In these and many other instances in this tradition, the guru is replacing the student's inner voice, their own discernment, and the system teaches total surrender and trust to the guru, to the Rinpoche, instead of the more empowering alternative of total surrender to our Highest Self and the Buddha Mind, the more empowering alternative of developing ever increasing discernment through meditation and trial and error to determine for our self what is best for us.

This spiritual tradition grew up 1000 years ago amidst a culture of caste systems, a master/slave mentality, and the Divine Right of Kings. The guru/disciple tradition in my mind represents the best possible application of a fundamentally flawed paradigm, that of master and slave. Similarly, killing people who are torturing and killing others is the best possible application of the fundamentally flawed paradigm we might call "killing human beings". But, at this particular moment in human history, in the awakening of human consciousness, we must take a non-incremental step forward and simply discard and stop living by fundamentally flawed paradigms. We can no longer get by doing the best we can inside of the wrong container. We must leave killing people behind, and we must leave master/slave mentality behind too, finding new and better models of human relationships we can use to preserve and pass on the sacred teachings of the Tibetans, as well as those of other ancient and profound spiritual traditions.

Returning to absolute and relative enlightenment—one of my acquaintances currently on retreat says that her

Reinventing Truth

teacher has instructed her whenever she is experiencing any sort of emotional difficulty in life, she simply should shift her mind into absolute consciousness. She indicated to me that this technique is very effective at relieving suffering in the moment, since she is no longer stuck in relative reality where the emotional pain and its "external causes" actually exist. The problem from my perspective however, is that always relying on this technique is a form of escape and it does not address the underlying issues. When we spoke she was struggling with some basic interpersonal dynamics with another student, and both of them were approaching the situation from a fairly immature level of emotional development. They were engaged in a drama and mutually reinforcing pattern that in my judgment would be befitting of young adults in their late teens or early twenties, not grown adults in their thirties with years of meditation and spiritual practice under their belts. The problem it seems is that their spiritual teachers are giving them the tools which they have, but which are not very well suited for dealing with ordinary reality and life situations. They are the tools of a monk wanting to disengage from the world and explore the edges of spiritual transcendence, not the tools of a person wanting to engage in ordinary life and develop life giving relationships and live a happy, well balanced life grounded in ordinary, normal reality, perhaps contributing to solving important practical problems that we humans are facing at this unique time in history.

I remember starving myself in a cave. I remember hating my wounded ego for acting out, hating myself for my weakness and inability to control myself. I remember putting the "spiritual" straight jacket on. I remember deep bliss and feeling immense joy in my heart too. Maybe sitting in a cave and putting the straight jacket on is what I most needed back then, or was the best I could do given the knowledge and resources I had available to me at that time. Maybe that was my Divine Path. Either way though, it was just one step on the path and did not get me to the imaginary end point. I still had and still have many steps ahead of me on the path to achieving full and abiding enlightenment in this cycle of growth.

I also remember only 9 years ago experiencing what I understand to be absolute enlightenment in a monastery in Burma where I was practicing a specific form of Vipassana meditation taught by Sayadaw Pandita. My experience was that of my awareness traveling from the surface of the earth—ordinary awareness—and digging down through layer after layer of dirt and rock—wounds and fears imprinted in my psyche and energy filed, and physically imprinted in my body—until I reached the core, the pure Light of my essence, my God-Self, and until I then pushed through the core into God consciousness, into absolute reality, into an experience of absolute enlightenment. I was surprised when God told me to leave that place and make the journey back outwards into ordinary awareness. I have been surprised at times since when I want to meditate to work through some difficult feelings, when the inner voice tells me, "No, you must stay and deal with these emotions at this level, not going deep inside to the safe and blissful place." At the same time, it all makes sense to me now, and it also makes sense to me that beginning two and half years after my experience in the monastery, that I spent five years working with a teacher/healer in England who was helping me work out and dissolve so many blocks in relative reality. Helping me use my experiences in business and in my personal life as doorways to go into the roots of the weeds showing up in my garden, and pull them out, or better yet transform them with my own compassion into new seeds, into seeds of the flowers which are just now finally beginning to grow and blossom in the garden of my life.

The beauty and awesomeness and complexity and simplicity of the path of my own soul and the broader process of consciousness unfolding through all of us—these are things I am grateful to have witnessed in this lifetime.

Absolute enlightenment came very quickly for me in this lifetime because in my case I had achieved it before. I was only in the monastery for 8 days, and it was on the 3rd or 4th day that I got to and through the core into absolute reality and God consciousness. Just as it only took me five and a half days to compose the first draft of Part I this book, what I thought was the whole book until just recently, and why now it has taken less than 12 hours to write this commentary section. Not only does this book build on my experiences and realizations I had during my life as Milarepa and in my life times since, but also I began having and writing down a number of the realizations outlined in this book even further back in the life of my soul, when I was an early author and spiritual teacher in the gnostic tradition.

When I went to the monastery 9 years ago, I had no idea that I had reached absolute enlightenment before, just as when I started writing this book I had no recollection of my lifetime in which I had written down a number of similar insights. I have found that often times in life we are not aware of the depth of experiences and strengths we are drawing upon when we are in alignment, nor do we appreciate the complexity and perfection of the puzzle that is taking shape in front of our eyes, as we surrender ever more deeply to our Highest Self and walk ever more discerningly on our Divine Path of full enlightenment and completion.

Commentary on chapter 16

I MADE THIS chapter intentionally short. As we near the end of this text, it is important that I leave more of the story untold, that I give you the opportunity to fill in more of the blanks on your own, so that this potentially new way of thinking about reality and looking at and challenging established spiritual teachings can take firmer root in your brain.

In this chapter I showed you the doorway and gave you a brief overview of the room inside, as opposed to going through a detailed description of all of its contents and how they all fit together. Hopefully, by this point in our journey together I have shared with you enough of my insights and perspectives, that when coupled with your own accumulated wisdom and experience, you are now able to more quickly and easily see through any number of other false realities, misapplied partial truths, or untruths and confusion posing as the Truth. Hopefully, as we near the close of this text, you are better equipped to see and avoid any number of other pitfalls you might encounter in life and with regards to any number of spiritual teachers and teachings.

For the sake of practice and/or future discussion and/or maybe just for fun, here are some other doorways you might want to explore, some other thought seeds to ruminate on by yourself or with some spiritual friends—exploring the implications of these truths for your life and the lives of others.

When we are not surrendered to our Highest Self and we are engaged in practicing manifestation techniques—such as those outlined in <u>The Secret</u>, any number of Law of Attraction books, as well as the books I recommend on this topic in Part I—when we are engaged in using our conscious intention to manifest things while not in surrender to our Highest Self, we are actually practicing a form of black magic, allowing our consciousness and human form to be used to bring in things that don't serve us or anyone else.

Following your bliss can get you into trouble.

If you are an individual going by an assumed and/or aspirational name—for example a woman who calls herself "Harmony" or "Joy"—now may be a good time to consider working through some of the issues associated with your birth name and your old life and personality. At some point on your journey—and maybe not right now—it will serve you to heal your wounded fragments and re-integrate, moving away from the dis-integration of a divided identity and back towards wholeness. The same is true if you are going by a spiritual name given to you by a teacher or one you have assigned to yourself.

Reinventing Truth

Sometimes dissolving pain through acceptance of reality as it is, is the path of the victim, the path of the weak and foolish. Sometimes we must draw a line and fight to change external reality into how we know it should be, relieving pain through changing the undesirable circumstances that are giving us accurate feedback—through the form of emotional and/or physical pain—about negative factors and forces in our environment and in our lives. Spiritual people must sometimes be spiritual warriors. Please do not use spiritual teachings to rationalize embracing the bliss of pain free acceptance when, in fact, it would be better for you and everyone else if you were to continue in pain, and fight.

Your "enlightened"/"spiritual" friends may be the enemy.

Sometimes resisting something doesn't make it stronger but sets you free.

Forgiveness is essential. Forgetting may not serve you.

It is important to be mindful of what we read and which meditations we listen to (and what we watch on TV, our iPod, the Internet, and at the movies too). Each time we interact with media of any kind, we are plugging into other peoples' mind streams and downloading all sorts of programs, many of which we may not want running on our system. Unless, of course, we have a well-developed, well-functioning anti-virus program installed and/or our system is so cleaned out that we are not vulnerable to most known viruses… in which case, it is still wise to be mindful.

Love everyone. Choose your friends wisely.

If our goal is full enlightenment, it is important that we don't allow our ego to identify too much with emerging psychic abilities, awakenings, or otherwise powerful spiritual experiences. While it might feed our self-worth to realize that we are an Angel living in a human body, it is important that we don't get so caught up in this experience that we hold our self back from becoming more evolved and enlightened than an Angel.

Why would anyone ever channel anyone else other than their Most Fully Conscious and Enlightened Self? Why would this ever be necessary or desirable?

Commentary on chapter 17

DRUGS AND SEX appear to be two of the most popular false paths. It is relatively easy for most people to see their addictions to alcohol or tobacco as addictions because they cannot point to a silver lining. Some people will try. Some alcoholics will point to the faulty science indicating that a glass of wine or two a day is good for you. Some smokers will point to Native American use of tobacco as medicine and in spiritual ceremony, indicating that even poison in the right hands can be medicine. Even so, most smokers and drinkers are not in denial that they are engaged in unhealthy, addictive behaviors.

It can be more difficult to be clear about certain drug-related and sexual experiences. There is in fact a healthy place for sex and sexuality in our lives, for example. Certain pathological behaviors around food and eating can be difficult to see for the same reason. We need food to live. There is a healthy version of eating and sexual expression, even though it is entirely certain that not all activities related to food and sex are healthy, and furthermore, that a great percentage of the Western world's population are engaged in unhealthy behaviors on a regular basis in these arenas. It is noteworthy that spiritual people who are healthy eaters can easily see how unhealthy most peoples' diets are, but if they themselves are engaged in unhealthy sexual behavior, they find it more difficult to see how unhealthy the sexual diets of many people are, both people in the mainstream and in the "modern spiritual" community. When people are engaged in unaligned sexual behavior, it is difficult for them to see the role of the craving center in the brain. It is difficult for them to see that they are spiritual thrill seekers engaging in exciting sexual activities or taking drugs or going to ecstatic dance class because they are addicted to the neuro-chemical experience these activities create. It is further difficult for them to see that the craving center has co-opted their spiritual journey to a meaningful degree, as well as in some cases the spiritual journeys of the teachers providing them experiences and techniques that unlock energies, create blissful highs and/or lead to perceived growth and transformation, but which are often times to a great extent really just keeping them stuck at the level of craving, trapped in the wrong container until they reach the point in their process when they decide to stop and meditate or otherwise become conscious and awake enough to see what is truly behind their actions – at which point they can choose to take a non-incremental step out of their craving center and into the next level of awakening.

The "spiritual" drug addict is frequently lost in any number of rationalizations that can be quickly overturned if you are able to have a rational conversation with them, if they don't somehow sidetrack or exit the conversation, or get upset and turn the tables on you to avoid having new

Reinventing Truth

layers of reality revealed to them that they might not want to see, or in fact, might not be ready to see yet. In many cases, what these people need more than reasoned arguments is the healing force of our compassion and their own compassion.

My former teacher in England, Clare, who asked me to refer to her only by her first name, taught me a very simple technique I will outline to you here, and which I may write more about some time in the future[31]. This simple technique is incredibly effective and powerful, and it is one of the keys to individual and planetary healing. She brought it in through direct realization, and I have been told of a couple others who have brought in through their own direct realization tools that may be similar in certain ways.

Whenever we are confronted with difficult emotions about any issue in our life, we can use them as a doorway to find the root of the issue and clear it out, to identify the karmic wound that is being projected onto the screen of our reality, so that we can heal it with our own loving and compassionate hearts.

If right now you are having trouble with your spouse or a close relationship, for example, I ask you to get really in touch with the emotions you are feeling and how that feels in your body. When you have gotten clear on this feeling, what you need to do next is start tracing it back through your memories until you can find the first and/or strongest experience of this feeling. Different memories and often times apparently unrelated situations will begin flashing across your mind. After all, we do have patterns that repeat themselves in different forms and contexts until we can get underneath them to the cause and get a shift. You should always be able to find a memory that occurred before the age of 16. If you have not, keep going back. Most of the time the root memory will be before the age of 11 and 12, and only every now and then will it be from early teenage years. Some times the root memory will lead you into a past life, but if you have not had these types of memories before, it is not very likely you would have one right now while reading this book.

Let's say the root memory was something that happened to you when you were five years old. If this is the case, you pull the five your old version of you out of yourself and sit him or her across from you. It is helpful if you are physically sitting somewhere with some space across from you, like on your bed for example, and then you visualize that there is a figure 8 drawn around you on the bed or wherever else you might be sitting. You are physically sitting in one side of the figure 8, and five year old you is in the other side. You ask the little boy or girl how they are feeling, either out loud or in your mind. It is helpful to keep your eyes closed. You will get an answer from younger you in your mind. You will be able to feel the presence of this consciousness sitting across from you as if it were a distinct individual separate from you and not a part of you, and he or she will communicate with you.

Most often you will get an answer like "I'm scared", "I'm ashamed ", or "I'm embarrassed." I'm angry. I'm confused. I don't know what I did wrong. I don't know why they are treating me this way. I'm tired. I want to die. Or something along these lines. Once you get three or four answers—sometimes requiring you to ask three or four times what else they are feeling—you can them give the younger you compassion for what they are experiencing.

Reinventing Truth

You don't agree or disagree with their experience, or try to explain how they misperceived reality or the situation. You are talking to a small child here and just giving them compassion for whatever painful experience they had. You picture sending heart energy across the figure 8 while saying out loud,

> "I'm so sorry you're scared."

> "I'm so sorry you feel ashamed."

> "I am so sorry you are angry."

> "I'm so sorry they treated you that way and you don't know why."

After giving them compassion for whatever it is they expressed, you check in with them again and ask how they are doing. You will likely find new difficult feelings below the first layer you just cleared out. Once you have a few more responses from them, you give them compassion again in the same manner outlined above. You repeat this process until you are done. By the end of the process you will either see a smiling little boy or girl sitting across from you, or you may observe in your mind's eye that their posture has changed and that they generally feel better, even if they are tired from processing these emotions and not expressing happiness in an obvious way. You will know when the process is done. At that point, it is good to either give the little boy or girl a hug, or hold their hands, or sit them on your lap, or dance with them, or do and/or say whatever else you are moved to do and/or say from your heart and which may be specifically consistent with some of the themes or issues that came up in your session (while refraining as much as possible from engaging the analytical part of your brain unless you are receiving clear guidance to do so from your Highest Self). During or following this step, this formerly wounded fragment of yourself gets integrated back into you. You have just cleared the negative imprint that was attracting difficult events into your life so you could see this wound, and now you have reinserted a healthier and happier part of you that will bring other benefits to your life. For example, you might find your healed inner child shining through in new and positive ways in certain aspects of your life going forward, and you will see quite clearly the situation in your life that prompted this exercise shift in meaningful ways and/or entire long-standing patterns or parts of patterns shift almost immediately.

During this exercise, it is optional for you to get up and actually sit inside the other side of the figure 8 physically, so you can feel in your body how that little boy or girl feels. You can do this if you wish each time before you are asking them how they feel.

Sometimes at the very beginning you might not get an answer because the little boy or girl is shut down or doesn't feel safe with you for some reason. This is a very literal situation and should be treated as such. Imagine if you were talking to a 5 year old child who didn't know you and who has just been through a difficult experience. If there is no answer, you might need to start with some compassion, to melt the ice enough just to get started. Common ones that work are,

"I'm so sorry you're numb."

"I'm so sorry you're shut down."

"I'm so sorry it's not safe to feel."

"I'm so sorry you are overwhelmed and don't know what you are feeling."

"I'm so sorry it's not safe to express your feelings."

Usually, one or more of these is enough to bring the child out of the deer in headlights stage and sooth them enough so they can communicate with you.

Also, there may be times you want to dig a little deeper on specific feelings that seem particularly charged. The child might tell you they hate themselves. In which case, you can go sit in the child and say over and over again, "I hate myself because…" You take off your mental filter and in a stream of consciousness say this again and again, just letting whatever words come out at the end of the sentence. You might find yourself saying some things that sound silly or odd, but almost always you will get some useful insights out of this process. You might find you hate yourself because you are ugly or stupid or evil or bad. You can then move back to the adult side of the circle and give compassion to the younger version of yourself, to your wounded fragment.

"I'm so sorry you hate yourself because you're ugly"

"I'm so sorry you hate yourself because you're stupid"

"I'm so sorry you hate yourself because you're evil"

"I'm so sorry you hate yourself because you're bad"

You might find you get some really powerful shifts getting even deeper into the feelings and also addressing the associated self-defeating belief systems that got anchored into your psyche back then when you were five years old. Clearing out these feelings and beliefs gets into some pretty deep re-programming that is highly beneficial. It's as if you are removing mental viruses or defragging your hard drive so to speak. Sometimes this is where past life events can pop through. You might find yourself saying. "I hate myself because I killed her", and it could be that you are referencing a past life event, which you may or may not remember. It is important not to judge what comes through in this type of stream of consciousness exercise or get too caught up in your rational mind wanting to know and understand more. Just give yourself compassion for whatever comes through. You will see through experience that this is the most important thing. Further insights and information will come to you over time at just the right time.

Once you gain practice with the overall method, you will find that you can skip the whole big process and give yourself compassion in real time, any time and any where, for difficult feelings coming up associated with specific situations in your life. You don't even have to trace back to root memories; you can just send the compassion inward articulating whatever difficult emotion you are experiencing. You can do this while driving in your car or in the middle of a difficult interpersonal situation, and you can see in real time how your outer world reflects your inner world. You will see how situations and even other peoples' behavior can shift, sometimes in real time right in front of you, as you clear out the wound, changing the scripts that are running them. In doing this you will gain an understanding of reality that can help you tremendously and be used to bring more healing into your life, other peoples' lives and the planet.

It is also very likely while on your healing path that you may have various psychic awakenings and develop various abilities, which again can be very beneficial for yourself and others, as long as you are surrendering ever more deeply to Divine Will and your Highest Self. If you are not surrendered in this way, it is very likely you are going to make some mistakes that will create some very bad karma for you and everyone involved. I abused my power in at least two lifetimes I can remember, and it is not a coincidence I ended up coming back two lifetimes ago as a powerless slave, that I had to endure all manner of suffering and abuse, both in how I lived and how I died. And all of these karmic imprints, both from when I was perpetrator and victim, have carried through into this lifetime and caused a great deal of pain and suffering for me up until this very moment. Karma is real, and it is extremely important that we make wise choices in our lives. That we make wise choices with regards to our thoughts, speech and actions. With regards to our intentions, where we put our energy, how we spend our time, how we earn, spend and invest our money, among other things.

I hope you will make better choices than I did back then and that you will act responsibly and with life giving intentions with the information I am sharing with you in this book. Information and power used properly can bring great joy into our lives and the lives of those we touch, but used improperly always leads to suffering for everyone involved. It is my greatest hope that you will surrender ever more deeply to your Highest Self, that you will receive and develop ever-increasing discernment and faith, and that as a result, all of your choices, all of your thoughts, speech and actions will be of benefit to you and all sentient beings.

Thank you for your work. Thank you for reading. Thank you for achieving Freedom and Enlightenment.

Epilogue

JUST BECAUSE SOMEONE has no individual karma does not mean they are free of collective karma. While it is true that when one of us becomes enlightened, we all do; it is equally true that for someone to become enlightened, we all must become enlightened. The process of consciousness unfolding includes a constant upward spiral of growth, in which various aspects of consciousness are bumping up against one another as the catalyst for continued growth for everyone involved. There is a spectrum of consciousness, a spectrum of vibration. If you are at the top of this spectrum, it does not mean you can't go higher, and the way you will go higher very well may be through your contact with consciousness at a lower vibration, e.g., people or other forms of consciousness who are not as evolved as you. You can clear out all of your individual karma, all of your family karma, all of your tribal karma, all of your race karma, all of your national karma, but still have species wide karma to contend with, still have consciousness wide karma to contend with. When I was fully enlightened some 25,000 years ago, I had no individual karma but I still had species wide karma that I was not aware of at the time because there weren't other people around to show it to me. There were few people and we did not have modern telecommunications and transportation technology. The world had not shrunk yet into the global village we live in today, in which our species wide karma is taking center stage and ready to be cleared.

I met a person once who in a past life lived on another planet. In that lifetime this person was fully enlightened and free of karma, and when I accessed their world through them, I could see and feel very clearly that this entire planet had no karma left, every being on the planet was fully enlightened and in a total resting state of peace and harmony. This individual told me that their species were somehow linked to ancient Egyptian culture and the pyramids, but they did not know much more. When accessing their planet and this alien consciousness, what came to me was that these highly evolved, intelligent life forms were linked also to the Tibetans—I, myself, recognized the specific imprint or frequency of this person's consciousness, their species' consciousness; it was like reconnecting to an old part of myself from my life as Milarepa, a part of myself that I had lost and forgotten about, until it literally just showed up in my field one day.

We know from chaos theory that reality is a series of microcosms within macrocosms, which are themselves the microcosm within a greater macrocosm and so on and so forth in a scaling function. I have had direct experience of my own past life as an enlightened individual free of individual karma but sharing species wide karma, and I have come across someone from a world free of its species wide karma but still sharing consciousness wide karma. My past self and that planet were in analogous stages of development and fit into their respective macrocosms in similar ways.

This individual is now here on Earth becoming more enlightened and continuing to grow as a result of living in a world that is at a lower vibration and level of consciousness than their former world. This person is dealing with new challenges, like adapting to a nervous system that is different than the one they occupied while evolving towards and later resting in a state of full enlightenment. Challenges like adjusting to a new and relatively hostile environment, learning how to show up as their Most Fully Conscious and Enlightened Self and help others do the same, even when surrounded on all sides by pathological behaviors and thought patterns, even in a lifetime when they were raised by parents and schooled by teachers that are less enlightened than their former self—essentially taking on some of our species wide karma as part of their continued growth trajectory and in an effort to help our species progress. New challenges like remaining humble and open to insights from others in spite of this individual's past and current levels of realization—a challenge that many highly evolved individuals may face from time to time.

As for me, I found this meeting to be both humbling and comforting, coming into contact with such a rare and special soul and realizing that consciousness from that planet has been intentionally pulling us up and supporting awakening on this planet for thousands of years. And even still, I find it both humbling and comforting to catch a glimpse into the broader process of consciousness awakening, a process that is much bigger and older than our human experience and life on this earth. I find it both humbling and comforting to develop a deeper understanding of The Nature of Reality and All That Is and to feel that much more connected with the One Consciousness that is underneath but even larger than human consciousness and earthly consciousness. I find it both humbling and comforting to feel that much more deeply the love emanating to us, through us, and as us—from the One Heart that is beating inside of us all.

Endnotes

1   I put the word healers in quotation marks because many people in the healing arts, myself included, feel it is not the right label to describe what it is that "healers" do. Most "healers" I know indicate that what they do is facilitate the person being healed in bringing about their own healing. It is the same person doing the healing and being healed; the role of the"healer" is to facilitate and witness. This definition, which is certainly more empowering for the "receiver", also has some problems of its own, which will be addressed later in this book. For the time being at least, it is important to highlight that the basic subject/object conception of healing is inaccurate, and as such, the basic subject/object nature of the English language leaves us with no word that I am aware of that is the appropriate, descriptive label for someone who engages in the healing arts, i.e., a "healer".

2   Of course, it was not "fate"per se, but rather the organizing intelligence behind all phenomena conspiring with my soul in order to bring this book in its current and exact form into being.

3   Please note. This is not a "Law of Attraction" or manifestation book. There are specific metaphysical principles including The Law of Attraction, which I cover in Chapter 1 because they are relevant foundation material to some of the topics I explore in this chapter and later in the text. If you are wanting to learn more specifically about manifestation, I would recommend two older works—Everyday Miracles: The Inner Art of Manifestation by David Spangler and Huna: the Ancient Religion of Positive Thinking by William Glover.

4   Many people believe that the soul cannot be wounded but is an unchanging, forever pure ball of light. Hindus share this belief and indicate there is a layer that is more subtle than the physical body but less subtle than the soul, the linga sharira, which is the "film" between the soul and physical reality, where we carry our karmic imprints between lives. Regarding many of the topics I cover in this book it is largely semantics whether the soul itself is wounded or if there is a layer between the soul and physical reality that carries wounds and karma. In some cases however, it is important to see the soul as something that changes and heals and unfolds through time and causation.

5   I realize that some spiritual traditions believe that if we are fully enlightened we would not be incarnate in physical form. This limiting belief system is an inaccurate understanding of Reality and All That Is, what Buddhists would typically call a "wrong view". I will return to this topic in the commentary section, but please don't skip ahead—it is best to read Part I in its entirety before reading Part II.

6   Again, there are relevant philosophical and/or semantic arguments here. Does your soul actually cause these things or is it your soul in cooperation with God, the organizing intelligence of the universe? For the current discussion, this delineation is unnecessary, since the key point is that the bad things are not causing the good things; the causal factors are hidden from our ordinary view and not what people often think they are.

7   In case it is not obvious based on context, I am not referring to the commonly held Christian notion of God—a personified God with human characteristics and feelings such as jealousy; a God that punishes, rewards, or intervenes in our lives in any way. I am referring to the Source of All That Is, the ground of creation, the organizing intelligence of the universe, the consciousness of which we are all a reflection of and part of.

8   Please note, this is not a silver lining—a good outcome in physical reality that we wrongly attribute as being caused by a bad thing happening in physical reality. This is actually the underlying reason of all phenomena in physical reality, the true reason behind all experiences. Everything does happen for a reason, just not the reasons we often erroneously conclude.

9   I refer to "typical" ego-identification and "current" ego perspective because as we heal our egos, deepen our surrender to our Highest Self and develop every increasing discernment—as we do these things, over time our egos can evolve and change shape to accurately encompass our soul and the experience of our soul, at which time ego perspective and soul perspective converge. Most people are not at this point in their journey, so for the sake of the cur-

rent discussion it is better to assume that soul identification and ego identification are two different things, even though they do not have to be. Furthermore, it is worth mentioning that the term ego-identification itself can be a little misleading. Our egos are the constructs that identify with things and gives us our sense of who we are—whether they are identifying with our souls or with dysfunctional thought patterns and emotions that don't serve us anymore. Whatever is in the container of the ego is what we think of us as our self, and since most people have a lot of dysfunction, woundedness and pathology inside of the container, what most people refer to as ego-identification can certainly be problematic. However, it's not that the ego is identifying with the ego—which is a little circular and confusing and which is why the term ego-identification can be mis-leading. It's that the ego is typically identifying with things other than the soul or our Highest Self, allowing these other things to control our thoughts, speech and actions—leading to negative consequences for us and everyone involved. More on these and important related topics is forthcoming in Chapters 6 and 8.

10   I use the word pathology frequently in this book and define it as any aspect of yourself that is out of alignment with or not an expression of your Highest Self; therefore any aspect of yourself that through metaphysical causation is drawing forth negative feedback into your life. I acknowledge this definition is broad and includes many thought and behavior patterns that would not be considered pathological from a clinical perspective.

11   Observational mind is the state of awareness where we can look at our self from outside of our self, observing

our body, our physical and emotional sensations, and our thoughts without actually identifying with them. Some teachers might make the analogy of a doctor viewing a patient—you see that the body is in pain for example, but you are not in the body, just a doctor objectively examining the body and noting the pain. It might also be useful to think back to the movie projector analogy. In this analogy, moving into observational mind would be moving your awareness into the audience and/or projection booth, watching the movie on the screen instead of being stuck inside of the movie as the main character with no awareness that it is just a movie.

12   When we see how this process is set up, it becomes clear that pain is not punishment and pleasure is not reward—a type of thinking many Westerners are prone to falling into based on the Judeo-Christian notion of a judgmental God. Instead, pain and pleasure are often forms of feedback that provide us with information about the negative or positive state we are in, so we can continue to consciously evolve and take further steps towards greater healing and enlightenment.

13   You may be wondering then where the wound originally came from. When did the cycle start? There is some content later in the book that sheds some light on this question. That said, it is important to be aware of when certain philosophical questions—such as this one perhaps—can be a distraction from the more important and basic realizations and healing work that needs to done at this point in our individual and collective journey. It is important to be able to discern the times when our curious minds are a part of the problem and standing in the way of our prog-

ress. Is your time and energy better spent right now thinking about this philosophical question or surrendering more deeply to your Highest Self, healing any wounds and clearing any karma that might be limiting your ability to do so?

14   Clearing karma is the same as healing wounds and becoming completely healed and whole on all levels. I briefly write about one way to accomplish these goals near the end of the commentary section. For more information on these important topics, I highly recommend the books Anatomy of Spirit: The Seven Stages of Power and Healing by Carolyn Myss, as well as The Twelve Stages of Healing: A Network Approach to Wholeness by Donald Epstein. Furthermore, as I suggest later in this book, it is worthwhile to seek out holistic practitioners who can help you with various aspects of your healing process. I found one of my most important healers/spiritual teachers in the Yellow Pages, in which she advertised her services as Integrative Bodywork.

15   I use the word addiction frequently in this book and define addiction as any ingrained pattern that repeats itself in your life without your full and conscious choice and which leads to consequences that don't serve you. Most obviously this can be thought of us things we normally think of as addictions, for example, an alcoholic drinking and getting drunk and engaging in destructive behaviors while intoxicated. My broader definition of addiction can also include patterns many people may not normally think of as addictions, patterns like "being squashed" by other people or repeatedly stumbling into and/or not leaving situations where you are unappreciated, taken advantage of or being abused physically or emotionally, for example. On some level even if your conscious mind considers these

experiences as negative and undesirable, your system is addicted to these experiences and the chemical processes associated with them, which is part of why it is hard to heal these wounds and shift these patterns. Part of your system is actually holding onto and addicted to your woundedness and your wounds playing out again and again.

16   Whether you are interested in exploring meditation for the first time or whether you already have a regular meditation practice, I highly recommend attending a 10 day Vipassana meditation retreat if you have not done so already. In 10 days you can accelerate the development of your consciousness by 10 years or more and transform issues that have been burdening you for 10 years or 10 lifetimes. Vipassana is a Buddhist meditation technique, but it is not necessary to change your religious beliefs or adopt any dogma in order to practice the technique. It is simply a means to develop and focus the mind's concentration, develop the ability to go into observation mind at any moment, and become conscious of chatter, obsessive thoughts and the likes and allow them to dissolve away, not letting them control your mind or body anymore. It is an incredibly powerful tool for attaining self-mastery and deep healing, as well as gaining wisdom and insight regarding whichever topics are most important to you. I have tried many, many things in my life, and Vipassana is in my opinion the single most important tool for attaining spiritual growth, deepening consciousness and achieving total healing. I cannot stress enough how beneficial it can be for the earnest seeker to attend a 10 day Vipassana meditation retreat. Vipassana is often referred to as Insight Meditation

in the West, and there are retreats held all over the world. You can find more information at www.dhamma.org.

17   For those on a spiritual path who were brought up Christian or Catholic or have otherwise been exposed to that notion of God in a very deep way, it may be useful for you to stay away from using the phrases Divine Will or God and instead stick to words like Highest Good, Highest Self, Most Fully Enlightened and Conscious Self, which may be less tainted by past beliefs and experiences. When listening for the voice that is leading you on your Highest Path, it could be confusing if you use words that have religious connotations or associations. All your collected experience and the experience of other religious people in your life can in essence create a "God entity" that is a type of consciousness that will communicate with you and try to guide you, but which in fact is not the real God, just a created entity that is the collection of all yours and many other peoples' associations with that word. Similarly for Buddhists (but perhaps less so due to differences in Buddhism and Christianity), it may be beneficial to steer away from the idea of the Buddha Mind for some period of time, and instead use new words without so many associations, because again the term Buddha Mind could be connecting you to and calling on a created entity that is not the essence of what you are truly seeking and trying to attune to.

18   Except, of course, for the times when there are simple rules, like "Thou Shalt Not Kill". The context with regards to what I am writing here is in reference to spiritual teachings and maxims, a great majority of which are an expression of one side of a paradox. In this context, there are no rules, because either side of the paradox is just partial truth,

Reinventing Truth

and we must discern in each moment what the best path is. I wanted to clarify this point, because taken out of context the statement, "there are no rules" could be used to justify all manner of pathological behavior, similar to some of the items I highlight later in the Commentary on the Introduction. There ARE some rules and principles we are always best served to follow.

19   For an excellent discussion of Lamarkian evolution vs. Darwinian evolution, please read The Biology of Belief by Dr. Bruce Lipton. I also highly recommend his audio recording series, which includes additional information and insights not included in his book.

20   While he is the greatest false light, he is not the only one. Please be aware of this and continue to develop the mental clarity and discernment to avoid falling prey to these dangerous and dark teachers, some of which may have best selling books and/or many thousands of students all over the world.

21   Breaking concepts is the basic concept of not allowing a single set of rigid beliefs dictate our behaviors at all times, i.e., altering our behaviors from time to time in a way that breaks any rules we have set forth for our self. Breaking concepts can be an extremely useful practice that helps us break through to the next level of realization, but like other concepts, it can also be used to self-delude and rationalize any number of pathological behaviors.

22   I have not heard or read any accounts indicating that physical violence and sexuality were combined in the form of sexual violation, but given even just the information available in the wikipedia entry on Osho, as well as my assessment of and familiarity with the mentality at play in

this situation, I strongly suspect that for a period of time sexual violation of varying degrees was condoned and did take place in the Osho Ashram in India—prior to the discontinuation of the entire practice of Encounter Groups and a public and published announcement by the Ashram indicating that these practices would no longer take place at the Ashram.

23   Tilopa was one of the great masters in early Tibetan Buddhism. Much has been written about him and his life. Almost any biographical sketch of Tilopa will include the fact that he practiced Tantra while working at a brothel, and will include a description of the famous "Sandal Transmission" he gave to his best known student and lineage holder, Naropa. The sandal transmission is the parable in which he essentially suggested Naropa make a Mandala offering out of Naropa's own blood and fingers, which Naropa proceeded to do by cutting off his own fingers before Tilopa hit him over the head with a muddy sandal at which time Naropa achieved enlightenment and his fingers were instantly healed. For those readers not familiar with Tibetan Buddhism, this parable may seem somewhat shocking, and perhaps it is not hard to imagine how earnest seekers could get confused and draw some wrong and distorted conclusions about the path of enlightenment based on these controversial behaviors of one of the key teachers and role models in Tibetan Buddhism. Tilopa is the founder of one of the four main lineages of Tibetan Buddhism, the Kagyu lineage, and he is considered by Tibetan Buddhists to be a fully enlightened master. Although he was a powerful and highly realized man—like a number of other great Tibetan Buddhist and eastern teachers—he was confused

Reinventing Truth

about The Great Deception and possibly other important points, and he was not at all times in surrender to his Highest Self, or the Buddha Mind. His confusion is evident close to a thousand years later in Osho's actions from sanctioning Encounter Groups to condoning prostitution as a means for people to support their spiritual pursuits financially to creating an amoral climate free of basic principles (i.e., concepts), a climate in which his followers could rationalize poisoning and killing people. It is for these reasons, I indicate that one could argue that Osho was an obscuration in Tilopa's mind stream.

24   Enlightenment then does not end cyclic existence, but is actually part of the cycle. The Buddhist Wheel of Life as I see it is a two-dimensional representation of a three dimensional spiral (viewed from the front or back, not the side), the spiral being a more accurate depiction of the path of consciousness unfolding, the path of our soul's journey to enlightenment and from one realization of enlightenment to the next realization of enlightenment further up the spiral. If the process of life were, in fact, a two dimensional wheel and we were indeed stuck running around in circles not getting anywhere while mired in never-ending suffering, it would seem wise to exit cyclic existence altogether by getting off the wheel, breaking the cycle. However, the Truth is that there is no way off the wheel; consciousness unfolding is a never-ending process. And, when we realize that life is not suffering but rather an unconscious life is suffering; when we realize that the further we get up the spiral the better things get, it becomes clear that we wouldn't really want to get off the wheel/spiral anyway, that the proper objective is not to exit the game, but to get further up

the spiral. It is best to exit unconscious cyclical existence, not existence altogether, which is by its very nature cyclical.

25   Or depending on how you look at it, his darkness kept him in this belief system to maintain control over him, used this belief system as one of its key hooks into him, as one of the key building blocks of the mental prison keeping him in servitude..

26   Which brings us full circle on the paradox of free will vs. fate. We do have free will, and our fate is to become fully enlightened through our choices. The specific form the path of enlightenment takes is up to us, and after the fact, it is easy to get confused and think that our specific path was fated because of the apparent logic of the progression of events and miracles that helped us along the way.

27   To me the whole idea of a spiritual persona is a bit of an oxymoron really, since so much of spiritual practice and development is about getting underneath persona and personality to what is real, but in the world of commercial spirituality and healing, it seems a widespread issue, an almost natural but not inevitable side effect to integrating the healing arts into a for profit, economic framework.

28   It is a classic example of "ends justifying means" type behavior, where people get lost in any number of warped rationalizations that enable them to do all manner of negative things under the cover of doing these things as the means to a positive end. This meta-trap—ends justifying means rationalizations—which takes form in a variety of different specific shapes in different circumstances is one more important pitfall we must overcome if we as individuals and as a species are going to find peace and happi-

ness in these bodies, on this planet. We must see that nothing good can come from bad actions, no positive ends can come from improper means. We can try to fool our self into thinking otherwise, but this is the Truth. Everything else is just self-delusion and warped thinking to justify taking actions that reflect our woundedness and keep us locked in unpleasant karmic patterns that don't serve us or anyone else.

29	Ending long standing friendships, getting a divorce, or quitting your job are all very serious life decisions. I do not take lightly mentioning these possibilities in this text, and at the same time, I do not want my writings to lead people to carelessly make huge life decisions based on waking up to how certain people or organizations draw forth negative aspects of themselves. It is important to realize that removing the stimulus and/or ending the relationship is just one viable approach to addressing the issue. It is possible sometimes to stay in the relationship and in the situation, while doing enough internal work to make major shifts so that you can show up differently, even if someone or something is actively drawing forth old, wounded aspects of yourself. Constructive engagement and total disengagement are both viable strategies. As always, I would argue that discernment and surrender to your Highest Self will be the keys to you successfully navigating these new awakenings and taking actions that are for your Highest Good and the Highest Good of all beings.

30	To some degree this is what effective healers and spiritual teachers do. In the first footnote in Chapter 1, I indicated that most "healers" I know indicate that what they are doing is facilitating the person being healed in bringing about their own healing. From this perspective it is the same person doing the healing and being healed; the role of the "healer" is to facilitate and witness. While this worldview is more empowering to the "receiver" and considered more politically correct so to speak within the healing community—this perspective—like it's less empowering counterpart in which the healer is healing the healed—is only partially true . It is also true that an effective and powerful healer can in some cases intentionally overpower important aspects of the receiver's reality and/or lend a powerful helping hand in supporting the "receiver" in shifting difficult aspects of their reality. An effective healer or teacher can shine their light so bright that they actually do melt away some of the darkness/bring more light into the fields of those who are in their orbit. Healers and teachers can and certainly do in some cases pull us up and/or partner with us to co-create new (and hopefully more positive) realities in our lives.

31   Since the initial drafting of this book, I have indeed written another book entitled Impossible Compassion, which is about how we can use directed compassion to bring about healing and transformations we might normally perceive to be impossible in our lives, the lives of others and the life of humankind.

ABOUT THE AUTHOR

EDWARD MANNIX HAS been on a conscious path of personal and spiritual development for over twenty years. He has practiced Vipassaana meditation in a monastery in Burma, travelled to Nepal to receive teachings and empowerments from Tibetan Rinpoches, and worked with hidden masters from a number of traditions and geographies, spanning Asia, Europe and the United States. Throughout his journey, Edward has consistently been focused on a form of practical spirituality—integrating his spiritual pursuits into ordinary life, not leaving worldly endeavors behind, but instead using them as a vehicle to go deeper into awakening. While on his conscious path and prior to becoming an author, he worked in the private sector as a management consultant and social entrepreneur. He holds an M.B.A. from Columbia University where he studied Sustainability and Social Enterprise, an M.A. from The School of Advanced International Studies (SAIS) at Johns Hopkins University, and a B.A. in Psychology and Economics from Indiana University. Drawing upon unique insight and an unusually diverse set of life experiences, Edward brings fresh perspective to ancient wisdom, and is emerging as an important new voice in the arenas of philosophy, spiritual development and personal transformation.